FIND YOUR VOICE AT WORK

The Power of Storytelling in the Workplace

Andrée Iffrig

Russ — trust stories from your personal and professional life will make a difference for others. Stories can be life changing.

Warmly,
Andrée

Library and Archives Canada Cataloguing in Publication

Iffrig, Andrée Eva
    Find your voice at work: the power of storytelling in the workplace / Andrée Iffrig.

Includes bibliographical references.
ISBN 978-0-9781037-0-5

    1. Storytelling. 2. Communication in organizations. 3. Leadership.
I. Title

HD30.3.I36 2007   658.4'52   C2007-901821-1

Limegrass books are available at special quantity discounts.

For details, contact:
Limegrass Productions Ltd.
Tel. 403-284-0639
info@find-your-voice.ca
www.find-your-voice.ca

This book is dedicated to my children.

For James, my favourite storyteller, who is given to hyperbole—
the world would be a poorer place without you.

For Heather, who understands that talk has to be accompanied
by action, and sometimes you have to act first
to prove your good intentions.

Table of Contents

Introduction

The Case for Storytelling in Organizations

"In the joy of the story, in the power of story, to create a world of power and joy for all living things."

Samy Weinberger a.k.a. Floating Eagle Feather.[1]

ADI WATCHES AS I LIFT THE PUPPETS from their brown paper wrapping. The top puppets have become entangled, their long limbs catching on each other. As I carefully separate one puppet from the other, disengaging their leather arms and buffalo horn handles, Adi names them for me: Arjuna, Krishna, Yudistira, and Srikandi. Each is a figure from the great Indian epic, *The Mahabharata*. At the bottom is the shadow puppet I have been looking for, the *Gunungan* or Mountain puppet. I place my hand beneath the puppet's flat body and extend it towards Adi.

The puppet's large size requires that Adi hold it to one side so that he can see around it. The Mountain is finely tooled in buffalo hide and painted with gold leaf. With the light behind it, I can appreciate the laciness of the tooling by a craftsman from Solo. The puppet has just arrived, part of a shipment I ordered after travelling in Central Java. Almost everything about this country has seduced me, from the puppet plays to the lilting sounds of Javanese gamelan music.

Adi Sasono is my boss at the Institute for Development Studies, a Jakarta-based non-government organization. Like most Indonesians, Adi is a storyteller, and as he admires the puppet it presents him with an opportunity for sharing a metaphor that will help me understand the Institute's work. I am new to the country and working as a western volunteer, supporting planning on a variety of community development projects. Indonesian culture in all its diversity is still a mystery to me. This is my memory of Adi's story:

The Javanese believe that all of us are on the Mountain, and walk it we must. The Mountain however is a dangerous place. Painted on the buffalo hide are wild animals representing the natural hazards that people will encounter. There is a sharp-toothed tiger and a crazed-looking water buffalo, horns down and pawing menacingly at the ground. The lurid pairs of eyes on either side of the puppet represent supernatural hazards that can harm or trap the unwary walker.

Right in the centre of the puppet is a red-faced, devilish-looking fellow called Banaspati. Both protector and destroyer in traditional Hindu mythology, he is the bearer of risk and danger and he represents an unpredictable and frightening source of power.

You might ask, "If the Mountain is such a terrifying place, how can you and I ever hope to reach the top?" The only way to ascend the Mountain is to walk together. Not only is it safer to journey as a community, but if one person falls or is hurt, there are others to stop and help her recover.

The shadow puppet's handle is crafted from buffalo horn, which has been straightened to make it easier to hold. Unlike this handle, the road to the top of the Mountain is not a straight line as people in the West so often think of it. It twists and turns along the climb. What counts is not getting to the top but the quality of the journey we make together.

The metaphor for the Mountain was told to me more than 20 years ago in Jakarta. My memories of where Adi and I were, or the occasion for our meeting are not sharp—was it just an encounter between the two of us, or were others present? I may have forgotten the backdrop but the details of the story are still vivid. Listening, I experienced an "a-ha" moment. In spite of our differences, I suddenly recognized that I belonged with the Institute's ragtag group of social activists, economists and community builders. Adi's story reminded me that the goals we shared were more important than our differences.

Does it matter if we tell stories? Yes, it matters! Think of the times you have heard a story, in a meeting or a coffee shop, and suddenly had your sense of purpose reaffirmed. Or the occasions another's story has convinced you that it was time to leave a personal or workplace situation no longer healthy for you. Or the stories that have brought you hope.

For several years now, I have sat in 12-step rooms with other people seeking to change their way of life, and it has been through listening to their stories of transformation and telling my own that I have found the strength to make much-needed changes. I have reached the conclusion storytelling is as essential for building strong communities as it is for moving through personal transitions.

If you care about the creation of vibrant workplace communities, this book is for you. You don't need a business card or a high-profile position to prepare you for becoming a storyteller at work. Anyone with the incentive to boost a team's morale or coach a colleague through a sticky transition can share stories.

Many management texts make storytelling sound complex. It isn't. If you wanted to become a polished speaker there would be a case for storytelling textbooks and extensive study. But the kind of storytelling described here is accessible to anyone with a capacity for honesty. By all means bring a sense of wonder, humour and courage to your storytelling, but don't worry about learning a variety of narrative techniques.

Some of the best stories I've heard have been remarkably "ordinary", presented without recourse to theatrical gestures or elaborate preparation. Their very ordinariness demonstrates how simple storytelling is. To earn a Ph.D. in storytelling, all you really need are some lessons in life, good intentions and self-awareness.

Stories draw upon personal experience and they engage our hearts. This is because stories speak to us at a feeling level, cutting through the coats of professional veneer that we accumulate working in organizations. You are more likely to remember a story than an email command issued from on high, and the chances of your "connecting" with a story of transformation are much greater than your responding to some well-reasoned analysis.

Collecting the stories for this book has been an organic process, much like storytelling itself. I never knew what would transpire during an interview. To my amazement, people told me unsolicited stories about themselves, about the struggle and challenge of being in business or serving in community, and about their own personal transitions. I am grateful for each interviewee's contributions and interest in storytelling.

USING THIS BOOK

As you read the following stories, I hope they trigger memories of stories you have shared with friends and colleagues. I invite you to join other storytellers online at *www.find-your-voice.ca*. Tell us about your failures and successes with storytelling in the workplace and community. Your experiences will enhance our understanding of story and how to encourage its use for others. You can expect to be inspired in turn.

Summaries at the end of each section capture the important points covered in the chapters for that section. Further individual and group course work is available online at *www.find-your-voice.ca.* The courses are designed to help you tap into your storytelling reservoir and to overcome the mental or emotional blocks you may experience in narrating stories at work.

As a weekly task, I invite you to begin collecting and recording stories, your own and other people's. Keep a notebook with you and begin to capture stories as they happen around you. Examples might include the excuse a colleague gives for being absent from work, the story you hear about a difficult customer, and the heart-warming tale of a challenge overcome.

The ascent up the workplace mountain is steep and the environment can be fierce. As Floating Eagle Feather says, story allows us to create "a world of power and joy for all living things." Let's share the journey together. ❧

Section 1

READER'S STORY

"Everyone has a story."

Neil LaBute - American director.

I F YOU ARE LIKE MANY PEOPLE, you will be scratching your head and wondering if you have any stories to tell. This assumes of course that you are already sold on the virtues of storytelling. Your experiences thus far may have been confined to bedtime reading as a child or with your child, or a humiliating memory of stage-fright. Perhaps you are suspicious of "storytellers" you have met in the past. These were people who blew their own horn or fabricated stories about how successful and proactive their leadership was, when in fact it was neither. We call these kinds of stories corporate myths, and they give storytelling a bad name.

Everyone has a story. I have several, and which one you hear depends on the circumstances in which I find myself. This does not mean I don't know who I am, or that I deliberately mislead people, only that I love stories and believe telling them is a path to self-awareness. In this first section, we explore story ideas for workplace settings.

In times past, ordinary people told stories in western society. Storytelling today is often regarded as the preserve of actors and professional speakers. The mass media supplies us with readymade stories which we watch for entertainment's sake. We believe them to be somehow superior to our own. Nothing could be further from the truth. As you read the stories in this section, search your life for stories, those that could bring hope to someone else. The rest of us crave inspiration for the journey, and your story may be just what we need to carry on. ❧

Engaging the World
through Story

"Stories are how we explain, how we teach, how we
entertain ourselves, and how we often do all three at
once. They are the juncture where facts and feelings meet.
And for those reasons, they are central to civilization—in
fact, civilization takes form in our minds as a series of
narratives."

Robert Fulford [2]

THE CITY BUS, A RICKETY VAN, jolts along a rutted road. The
van's paint has faded, the interior upholstery is torn in places
and if this vehicle ever had shocks, they are now long gone. We are
in Bandung, a city three-hours drive south of Jakarta, and not only
are the roads in bad repair, but there are 16 of us jammed into a
12-passenger space. I feel like a big, white whale in a sea of brown
bodies. No sooner am I seated than the questions begin.

"Ibu, (a polite way to address a married woman), what is your
name? Where are you from? Do you have children? How many
years have you been married? Why are you here?" I try to respond
good-humouredly to the interrogation. My name is Ibu Andrée and
I am from Canada. I am here in Bandung to study Indonesian; in
another month or two I am moving to Jakarta to work in a community development organization. All ears have tuned in. These
people want to know my story.

My marital and familial status is far more important than my academic degrees. The conversation abruptly halts when I mention that after 12 years of marriage, I still have no children. This news is incomprehensible to my fellow passengers for whom children are the fulfillment of life's purpose. One by one, my listeners tell me their stories: how many children they have (quantity counts), whether they have always lived in the city or come from the countryside.

This bus episode will be repeated many times over during my stay in Indonesia. In government offices and farmers' fields, people tell me their stories and ask me for mine. Indonesia has an oral culture. People's lives seem to unfold as a series of stories. Wanting to fit in, I begin to record the narratives I hear and to tell stories myself.

Now working as a curriculum designer and facilitator for communications training, I am convinced that adults learn best when their hearts as well as their minds are engaged. Some of my clients inform me that they *only* learn when their hearts are engaged. I can't hold people's attention with dry facts but they do remember stories, their own better than mine. In our sessions together, participants have plenty of time to share these, to reflect on their experience and reframe their perspective.

It is not uncommon for me to meet with employees and managers who feel discouraged. In coaching sessions one-on-one, I ask them to tell me their stories and together we explore what they can learn from these narratives. I hear the same refrain at every coaching session and course I facilitate: participants don't feel they have a voice at work. When we do some digging it transpires they have been stifling their voice rather than standing up for their values. The answers to their challenges are inside them, if only they had the courage and time to access this tacit knowledge and experience.

We engage the world through story more than most of us recognize. Every time you encourage someone at work it is an occasion to tell a story. When the team is faltering, a story can help. Storytelling provides a more subtle and convincing method of winning support for your initiatives than simply telling people what you want them to do.

Our lives in community are rich with stories. Think of all your stories from coaching kids' sports teams or fighting City Hall. Reflect back on the times your team or neighbourhood organization was unsuccessful in raising funds or achieving a particular goal—these tales can be powerful.

Sometimes story is a way to provoke others to explore an issue. It is a technique that religious teachers have used for millennia and it still serves a useful purpose today. When people gather to study ancient texts, the teacher (rabbi, imam, pastor, priest, spiritual leader) asks provocative questions in association with a time-honoured story. The group learns through debate and more storytelling. You can apply the same approach with a learning forum in a workplace or community venue.

We find healing by telling our stories, whether in the privacy of a therapist's office or in the context of supportive community. Self-help groups of all kinds are a testament to story's power. Hope is reborn when people gather together to share in this way.

To say you have no reason to tell stories is to overlook the ways in which you are already engaging the world through story. The value of storytelling may not always be appreciated, and the average workplace can seem particularly insensitive, but we need stories more today than ever. They are how we relate to other people, how we work our way through transitions, and how we entertain each other in the process. They are, as author Robert Fulford points out, the juncture where facts and feelings meet. ❧

What is My Story?

"Story is one of the most potent containers for meaning."

Interview with Rachel Naomi Remen. [3]

IT'S A CURIOUS THING, but if you've made no mistakes—or at least none that you'll own up to—you will probably make a lousy storyteller, and the stories you do narrate will be unlikely to resonate with your listeners. They want to hear real stories about steep-hills-to-climb and mistakes-made-and-lessons-learned. Your listeners will be more entertained by a story of resistance and defeat than a slick narrative that makes you sound perfect.

Adi Sasono's story of the Mountain puppet enabled a foreign volunteer like me to appreciate the work of his agency in Indonesia. The Institute for Development Studies was embattled at the best of times. Like most non-profits, it was chronically short of funding. Its situation was further complicated because it challenged the dictatorship of Soeharto by building stronger community networks. Soeharto's government did not tolerate cooperative organizations outside officially-sanctioned bodies, fearing these would lead to unrest and the reawakening of communist sympathies.

The Institute used story to affirm its purpose, encourage its supporters and clarify its role for communities where it was engaged in development work. Many of these stories illustrated the agency's struggles rather than its successes. What these narratives demonstrated beyond a shadow of a doubt was the Institute's dedication to improving the lot of poor Indonesians through participatory means.

Similarly, your story is a way to explain your sense of commitment to people you work with. It might be a narrative you share with a protégé, a colleague, or someone higher up in the organization.

Story is what happens when people gather together and talk. It is not always "positive" in the sense of affirming the organization's agenda. Perhaps your story is one of rebellion, of changing the status quo, of leaving unhealthy circumstances and striking out anew. Your story may be one of brokenness, of coming to terms with your losses or less than perfect actions. Your story may be inconclusive—a story of a situation not yet resolved.

Your story is at once timeless, because all story reflects a wider human experience, and exclusive, a result of your personal experience. Your story is unique to you, and yet others listening may hear some of their own story in yours.

Most of us have several core narratives we could tell. I have been a victim, survivor and hero. I have been cared for and a caregiver. I have been an adventurer, and I also know what it's like to feel trapped with no way out. I have been a saint and a sinner. The story I narrate depends on my perspective during any given circumstance. All of my stories are valid for me.

Your story is not how successful you have been, and it is not necessarily work related, although you might tell the story at work. It's not a script for entertaining the troops. That's theatrics, not storytelling. And it is not a way to promote the organization; that's marketing. No, the kind of story referred to here is a snapshot of the experiences you have had and their meaning for you.

It is the story you would tell if your work group was demoralized or if you felt wronged and were struggling to understand how you had come to this impasse; it is the tale you would share in a coaching session to provide direction and encouragement; it is the metaphor you would relate if your organization had just been turned upside down by a change in leadership.

Everyone has stories to share for circumstances just like these.

Let's take my part of the world as an example. Where I live, the oil and gas bonanza has made for rapid economic and demographic growth. Simultaneously, there has been sweeping organizational change. Workplaces are stressed with chronic change initiatives as companies introduce large-scale upgrades of software systems or new customer service processes. People are being asked to work longer hours either because companies can't find skilled labour or because the bottom line dictates greater economies. Many employees have the unsettling feeling that no one in upper management really knows what's going on, and transitions don't go nearly as smoothly as leadership promised. Community organizations like hospitals, schools and social service agencies are stretched to the hilt as well, trying to address the human challenges that go with breakneck growth and budgets never generous enough.

All this change is difficult. What story could you tell to connect with others caught in the crossfire?

Much depends on how you see yourself. If you feel like a victim, your story will focus on circumstances beyond your control. Management will be cast as the thoughtless, heartless instigator of poorly conceived initiatives. If you are a rebel, the villains of your tale will be the civic bureaucracy or the corporate world. If you see yourself as someone who has survived repeated change initiatives, your message will be either one of hope (I made it and am a better person for it) or deep cynicism (They haven't done me in yet!). At the other end of the scale is the narrator who has been responsible for organizing change and believes fervently in the need for yet more; his story will focus on the benefits for all.

There is value in each of these narratives. One is not better than another—that's not how story works. Assuming you are being genuine, your story simply provides your understanding of where you are now. It is a bridge to those you work with and a jumping off point for finding resolution together.

My wish for you is that as you explore your past for story content, you will do so with wonder, not disgust. Be generous with yourself. Strike out in search of narratives that reflect your values and how you have changed. And be open to other people's stories and experiences that differ from yours. You will be amazed to discover how storytelling—and listening too—provide one of the most powerful development exercises available. ❧

Does My Story Matter?

"Without a sense of caring, there can be no sense of community."

Anthony J. D'Angelo.[4]

O N MAY 16, 2006, the day after mountaineer David Sharp died on Mt. Everest, I met with a client in his Calgary offices. "Frank" is a manager with an oil and gas transmission company. He is also an ardent mountaineer and cross-country skier. David Sharp's story was headline news that morning because while succumbing to high altitude sickness at Everest, he was passed by at least 40 trekkers en route to the summit. No one stopped to bring him back down the mountain.

As we took our seats for a pre-arranged meeting, I asked Frank what he would have done in circumstances like those faced the previous day by the Everest climbers. Would he have stopped to assist Sharp, maybe even turning back to get him to safety, or would he have continued on to the summit? Frank's perspective was important to me. The actions of the mountaineering community at Mt. Everest were weighing heavily on my mind.

Frank paused before answering. Then he told me this story.

Frank has led a variety of backcountry trips, including trips to some of Canada's highest peaks. A handful of attempts at some of these peaks were foiled by bad weather or illness. Other mountaineering teams braved the weather, but as the leader for his trip, Frank didn't want to put other people's lives at risk so that he could summit.

On one of these occasions while preparing for the final push to the top, a member of Frank's group began to exhibit signs of altitude sickness. Knowing the results could be life-threatening without immediate medical attention and descent to lower altitudes, Frank turned his team back. That same day, another expedition on the same mountain also had a sick member in tow. That team elected to leave their team-mate behind for the time it would take them to reach the summit. When they returned 90 minutes later, he was dead.

Having shared this story, Frank was silent for a while. Almost as an afterthought, he added: "It's about the journey, not the destination."

Unwittingly, Frank had just convinced me of his courage, compassion and integrity. A friend of mine says that integrity means that you are the same on the inside as the outside. Frank exemplifies this inner/outer continuity. He is the kind of manager most employees would love to work for. Whenever I doubt leadership's capacity for integrity, I will remember this story.

Frank isn't given to blowing his own horn, and he would be amazed if someone told him he is a born storyteller and leader. Yet his words that morning in May 2006 continue to inspire me, reminding me that how we choose to live together in community is vital to our wellbeing and sense of self. "Turning back from the summit" is Frank's story, and it mattered to me. ❧

Self-Limiting Beliefs

"With everyone's stories swirling so bewilderingly around us, it is little wonder that many of us feel we are losing touch with the richness of our own."

Gary M. Kenyon and William L. Randall. [5]

WHEN I MEET PROSPECTIVE CLIENTS, I review my "credentials" with them—other clients I've worked with, stories of my success with communications planning, the presentations I have given. This tells them some of what I do, but it gives them no sense of who I am. I could just as easily tell stories about raising a seriously ill child or volunteering as an art educator in the public school system. Those stories speak more to who I am, but somehow they don't seem so germane. I worry they diminish me in a corporate environment. This fear of mine reflects a self-limiting belief that runs contrary to the spirit of storytelling.

There is a misguided notion in business circles that you have to look polished to progress. No one wants to hear about your detours. Job applicants who are well prepared for interviews have carefully concocted stories to make themselves look good in front of interviewers. After all, if you really knew me would you still want to hire me?

The belief that I can only share stories that put me in the most flattering light is a two-edged sword. Once I create this impression, I am bound to live up to it. It is exhausting and stressful to be on my best behaviour all the time and inevitably, like the Prima Donna who loses her cool right before curtain time, I will betray myself by being human. You might come to the conclusion that no one could really be that wonderful anyway, in which case I have blown my credibility from the get-go and failed to achieve my ends.

Thinking back to people's stories that engendered my respect, it wasn't the perfect stories but rather the imperfect people who interested me. I listened avidly to the details of their missteps and the tangle of emotions they experienced in extricating themselves. There was a sympathetic connection that happened as I recognized myself in their stories. I have learned that when I am honest about my mistakes and some of the messier bits in my life, my listeners are surprisingly receptive. Sometimes, we laugh together at our mutual foibles. This is true for stories narrated during formal presentations, and it holds for informal circumstances like coffee dates and meetings.

What about the belief that storytelling is for professional speakers, marketing coordinators and senior executives, not for mere mortals like the receptionist or Help Desk crew? If you wait until you're old and grey or more highly placed to tell stories, you may never become comfortable sharing them. I have been inspired by illiterate farmers in Java and people fresh from living on the street in urban centers in North America. In fact, I sometimes think people who have known real hardship have more to teach about hope and life-on-life's-terms than any CEO. Storytelling, the kind that changes lives and makes people willing to work through difficult transitions at work or in community, is not the preserve of the high and mighty or the well-rehearsed.

If you have ever been ridiculed for telling a story, by a teacher, parent, partner or manager, the prospect of further sharing will strike fear in your heart. It takes courage and determination to overcome put downs. And even if your story is genuine and delivered with good intentions, not every listener will like what you say. In my industry there is a rule of thumb that says 15% of the audience is always going to be critical, no matter how good you are. The fact they dislike your presentation is often a reflection of who they are and not what you said.

If this is true for speaking and facilitating, it is probably safe to assume that some critics from your past were more uncomfortable with themselves than with your story. In narrating a heartfelt story that awakens people's feelings, you connect with them at a deeper level. This makes some listeners uneasy: they don't like to feel or show emotion in a professional or public setting. Often it is the people who are closest to us who struggle most with our storytelling. Pandering to their sensitivities will only silence you and drive your stories and feelings underground.

Any belief you hold that keeps you from sharing what matters to you is not serving a useful purpose. Through story, you can honour your experience in life. ✖

Real Stories from Real Managers

"Learning to speak with a human voice is not a parlour trick."

Excerpt from *The Cluetrain Manifesto, www.cluetrain.com.* [6]

ARNE IS THE HARDWORKING MANAGER for one of the district offices of an oil and gas supply company. He lives in a small town in northern Alberta and manages several sales people and administrative staff. On the day I catch up with him, he is shaking his head over one of his sales representatives. The man is technically competent but unfailingly disorganized and prone to miss reporting deadlines. Arne has to produce a monthly report for head office in Calgary, and this man's disregard for deadlines and reporting is a source of constant friction.

So far, this is not a very remarkable story.

I begin our interview by asking Arne to speak to a time when he overcame a challenge at work. The plan is to use his story for the company's in-house newsletter. Arne has a reputation for being a raconteur and for successfully landing new business. I expect him to entertain me with a winning story about a fat contract he signed for the company, or the time he figured out an artful way to deal with a client's pipeline problem. Reflecting for a moment, he describes instead his current difficulties with the wayward sales rep.

Despite numerous attempts, Arne has failed to motivate this man to write his reports in a timely way. Suspecting this employee is feeling intimidated by the boss's direct approach, Arne recently decided to ask for help from staff. As Arne likes to say, he may be the district manager but everyone works as a team. The district's office coordinator has earned the respect and trust of the sales rep, and so it has fallen to her to educate him in the finer points of meeting deadlines and preparing reports using the company template. They have an agreement that she will monitor his progress and provide additional support as required to keep him on top of the reporting process.

The verdict is still out on the future of this sales rep with the company. Arne tells me he would like to avoid firing the man, who is otherwise a competent employee and decent person. In explaining his own inability to deal with the employee, Arne has overlooked all he has accomplished. By reaching out to his staff for assistance, he is making the most of the inherent strengths and talents of each team member. Not only will the sales rep get the help he needs, but the whole office will be stronger for strategizing to support a fellow employee.

Listening, I am impressed by this manager who is willing to own up to his own inability to engage an employee. As a consultant investigating the company's progress with a knowledge sharing initiative, I have learned more from this account than if Arne had related a typical sales success.

Arne's story sticks with me as an example of a real story from a real manager who does not always have answers for what life throws in his path. In my mind, Arne is the prototype of an exemplary manager—devoted to his community, concerned for his employees, willing to acknowledge his shortcomings and determined to make the company a success. No wonder he tells good stories! ❧

Is It Safe to Share My Story?

"If you can't get through, walk around."

Finnish proverb. 7

W E WERE HALFWAY THROUGH a teambuilding seminar and discussing how participants would apply the concepts. I could feel an uncomfortable silence descend on the room as we explored ways to challenge management practices that undermined team cohesiveness. The class was composed of 18 banking industry employees, and the prospect of finding their voice at work was intimidating.

After some hesitation, first one participant and then another explained why it wouldn't be safe to speak up. Apparently their managers ate employees for breakfast. A third person remarked somewhat sarcastically that if anybody needed this teambuilding course, it was the managers. In the dialogue that followed, I encouraged them to step over the boundary created by their fear. I used my own experience to demonstrate the rewards for doing so. I'm not sure I convinced them.

Ridicule is hard enough to deal with, but jeopardizing your job is another matter. Many of the participants felt that it was too risky to be honest with management. Listening to their concerns, I had the impression they live in a world where everyday at work feels insecure. Change means they do not know if they will keep their jobs, and the prospect of banding together to improve the atmosphere at work seems daunting. I was reminded of the ancient Israelites who wanted freedom but were afraid to leave a familiar slavery in Egypt.

There are some wonderful stories of working through fear in John Kotter and Daniel Cohen's book, *The Heart of Change: Real-Life Stories of How People Change Their Organizations.*[8] My favourite is about a senior military official in post-apartheid South Africa. In the face of hostility from other officers, he stands up for what he believes in: the creation of a mixed-race army representing the values of the new country. It is a riveting story and a great example of the stages of teambuilding; the participants in my workshop were deeply moved by it.

Some organizations do not feel like safe places to be real, especially if there is a critic present. Nowhere is it written that you can't tell stories informally in your work groups, away from the critics—tales to encourage your team-mates and overcome fear. Even managers with hairy manes need to hear real stories of people who have made a difference. If you tell stories often enough, your managers might even acquire some storytelling skill themselves.

With storytelling, you don't point fingers. Instead, you ask your listeners to step into the narrative and consider how it applies to them. This is less coercive than a more direct approach, and it gives listeners time to absorb your message. If one of these workshop participants were to narrate the Kotter and Cohen story from South Africa, peers and managers alike would discover the meaning it held for them. Even the most intractable manager would have an uncomfortable moment recognizing herself in the narrative. It might be the incentive she needed to change.

Participants left the teambuilding seminar with a detailed template for building a strong team. It included identifying leaders in the wider organization who would champion the team's mandate and work to overcome resistance from management. As I left I noted the air of despondency had lifted slightly. I don't know how many participants will have actually put the template into action, but they were certainly clearer about the value of storytelling.

Fear kept me from telling stories for a long time. Growing up, I was ridiculed by family members if I shared what I felt. Today I understand they had too many emotional wounds to be generous with me. I have learned to name the fear, allow it in the room and either challenge it or walk around it.[9] Refusing to acknowledge fear is counterproductive and generally makes the situation worse. ❧

Cathi's Story

"The stories that touch us—child and adult—most deeply are, like our myths, crafted visions, shaped dreams. They are not the smaller dreams that you and I have each night, rehearsals of things to come or anticipation/dread turned into impenetrable symbols, but the larger dreams that belong to all humankind, or as the Dream Weaver says, 'The heart and soul made visible.'"

Jane Yolen. [10]

I HATE SHOPPING, AND I AM A FOOL about buying clothes—I would be lost without Cathi. She manages the women's department of a successful clothing shop that is locally owned. She has a great customer ethic and seems to genuinely enjoy making women like me look good.

Here is one version of Cathi's story: She is an astute business woman with an enviable track record in her industry. She is a talented manager with a good eye for fashion. She makes a good return for the shop's owners.

Somehow, this story seems impoverished. Perhaps I should tell you that she came up through the ranks in the fashion trade. Cathi is determined and hardworking. She is a wife and mother to two children, and makes balancing her professional and work lives a priority.

Recently, I asked Cathi about her summer plans. She broke into a broad smile and told me about the family's upcoming trip to Africa. Her daughter's elementary school has been involved in a global education project with a partner school in Litein, Kenya, and Cathi's family has been one of its biggest supporters. Curious about conditions at the African school and looking for more ways to champion the project, Cathi and her family decided to spend their vacation in Litein.

As I continued to ask questions, I learned that her daughter Samantha while still in Grade 2 was an instigator in the creation of a musical CD and video about the partnership. With leadership from a local real estate agent who is also a musician, Jeff Rolheiser, the CD features choirs from the African Inland Church Children's Home in Litein and Fred Seymour School in Calgary. As the story of the partnership has spread, other humanitarians in the city have become involved with the project. Ironically, Fred Seymour School has since been closed by the school board, but Cathi's family continues to enthusiastically support the children's home in Litein.

Could I buy the CD? Yes, she had some behind the counter. I went home, slipped the CD into the computer and wept as I watched the video, a testament to children and parents in a North American city working together to make a difference in a village struggling with the effects of poverty and AIDS in Kenya.

Let's rewrite Cathi's story. I'm not sure she would choose to tell it like this, but this is how I see her.

Cathi makes me look beautiful. She is a successful fashion manager with a big heart. She works for a family-owned firm in Calgary that is part of our community. Her family wanted to help children in Africa get a good education and better health care. They have been helping to raise awareness and funds for a Kenyan partner school through a heart-warming CD of songs recorded by children in Litein and Calgary. Cathi sees her family's current involvement as just the beginning of what they can do to make a difference in Litein. By sharing her story with a business client like me, she gave me a chance to make a difference too. That's what sharing stories is all about.

If you want to learn more about the Fred Seymour Elementary school project go to: *www.keepingthecirclestrongfilm.com*. ❧

Private versus Public Stories

Leaders are real people with families, problems, hopes and dreams.

W E ARE SEATED AT A SMALL TABLE in an East Indian restaurant. My companion has her back to the door, open in mid-summer to the rush-hour traffic outside. Chris has been asking about my family and work, catching up since we last met six months ago. In between crunching on fiery-hot wafers called papadums, I inquire about her life. Smiling ruefully, she tells me about the family's decision to invite her oldest son and his pregnant girlfriend to move in with the rest of the household. These young people seem hardly ready to start a family of their own.

I detect a softening in her face as she describes what holding her first grandchild has been like, this perfect little human being with tiny fingernails and amazingly soft skin. She reminds me that her own children were adopted, and this is her first experience of caring for a newborn. It was a little intimidating at first. She paints a picture of getting home from work to go for a walk with the dogs, the baby tucked into a carrier on her chest. I can hear the wonder in her voice.

Chris is a competent professional, a director with one of the largest community development organizations in the city. I have not seen this side of her before. The story of housing her son and his girlfriend fits seamlessly with her professional work, overseeing policy development and projects to reduce poverty and help the needy. In relating this story of a family pulling together to help its most vulnerable members, she has let me into her world and affirmed what really matters to her.

Unwritten rules about public communications hang invisibly on office walls. Be businesslike. Don't let people find out about your mistakes. Don't let them see your fear. Don't talk about faith and don't get too personal. Be a cool grownup.

Repeatedly I have seen this advice ignored by intelligent adults who felt it was worth taking a risk to share a personal story. There are places and times when it is less appropriate—a financial meeting for instance. Even in these I have seen a speaker break the rules and share a private moment to connect with his listeners. When you speak to your deepest values, you touch other people's hearts. ✀

Not Every Story Is A Fairytale

"He seemed to do very little except listen to her. But he listened in a way she had never experienced. She heard herself in a new way. She began to hear her own voice, not the voices of others. She began to understand what she was doing because she had not believed in herself."

Warren Redman. [11]

I HAVE MISGIVINGS about this interview. The employee who arranged it was cagey about the reasons for meeting one of the staff in the accounting department. My task is to interview people from all over the organization, focusing on how people are adjusting to rapid change. There's some mystery surrounding this particular encounter that I don't quite grasp, as though there were an ulterior motive for my meeting with this colleague.

Thus I find myself one morning in an office with an employee whom I'll call Mary; she seems unusually reticent and ill at ease. In an effort to make her more comfortable I begin with some pleasantries and inquire about the nature of her work. She is brief with her answers. Unlike other employees I have interviewed, Mary is wary and distrustful.

I believe that being present and not interrupting is one of life's greatest gifts. Interviewing requires deep listening, and gives permission for silence and a variety of emotions to enter the room. I listen respectfully to Mary's answers and only ask questions to clarify and move the story along. When I ask her about a challenge she has faced recently, she gradually unfolds this story.

Mary has been with the firm for several years in a business and administrative function. To further her career, she completed three years of night classes in the accounting area and is close to achieving certification. A new manager for accounting was hired a few months previously and Mary was asked to focus on payroll, a mundane aspect of operations. She felt relegated to doing a task she no longer enjoyed and thwarted in using her new skills.

The new manager is not what he appears to be. With the CEO he is charming, but working with the staff he picks scapegoats. Mary is his prime target. Systematically, Mary has found herself either being isolated from the others, or made an example. In one episode the manager humiliated Mary by obliging her to take a week off work without pay; this was a penance for failing to complete work according to the manager's timeline. Mary felt demoralized and her treatment has cowed the rest of the staff. Given this manager's chummy relationship with the CEO, it seems to Mary there is nowhere to go for help.

It's a long interview. As she tells me her story, I can hear Mary moving from anger at her treatment to recognition that by failing to stand up for herself, she has invited more abuse. Gradually, she names her frustrations and the fear that has kept her isolated. Sharing her story in a safe place with someone she can trust to listen and not judge is freeing her from fear.

This story has a happy ending. As a result of our interview, two days later Mary found the courage to share the story with the CEO. A seasoned veteran of the financial services sector, he told me that after hearing the details of her story, he went into the bathroom to throw up. The offending manager was fired, and Mary has learned to stand up for what matters to her.

My only task as Mary's listener was to be a witness to her struggle, without stepping in to "fix" her or tell her what to do. Mary had the answers inside her; she just needed a chance to get them out. Not every story is a fairytale, but all stories are equally instructive and valid. Sharing her private story was the beginning of her healing. By telling it, she discovered she was part of a caring community. This is the beauty of storytelling, even a story of suffering. In telling and in listening, we discover we are one. ❧

Summary 1

1. Storytelling is a way to reclaim your voice at work.

2. Workplace storytelling is meant to be genuine and provides an understanding of where you are, warts and all.

3. Your story matters, however ordinary or insignificant it may seem to you. Telling it could encourage or enlighten those around you.

4. Resist the urge to make yourself look good in stories. Your listeners can't connect with someone perfect, and they may become suspicious of your stories.

5. Narrating stories can be scary and requires taking risks. Learn to name the fear and then walk around it.

6. Every time you share a heartfelt story, you enrich another's life and give that person a chance to make a difference, too.

7. Sharing your story at work brings you into community. In telling stories and in listening to others' narratives, you discover you walk on common ground.

Section II

The Sound of Story at Work

"... a culture of storytelling is one which encourages the collection and sharing of knowledge in conversations."

Excerpt from *www.cluetrain.com*.

YOU ARE SITTING IN A JOB INTERVIEW, and the interviewer says, "Tell me about a time you had to overcome resistance to one of your ideas." As the interviewee, your task is to spin a story that puts you in a good light.

In a performance review, your boss asks, "How did you solve that problem?" If your performance is being criticized, the question might be, "Why aren't you meeting deadlines?" Either way, the question elicits a story.

In this section, we explore the sound of story at work. Storytelling is more widespread in organizations than many people realize. Project debriefings bring together team-mates for post-mortems on what worked and what didn't work. During these occasions you'll hear the raucous din of war stories describing obstacles the team overcame, or the tuneful expression of gratitude for support from allies in the organization. Client meetings rarely end without a tale demonstrating your competencies as a service provider. Depending on your delivery, these stories may sound sincere or ingratiating to your audience.

Story is productive for sharing, creating and spreading new knowledge in an organization. The hum of informal exchanges can be heard throughout the day, as a manager or mentor instructs an employee, or employees gather for a team meeting. After-work get-togethers at bars and coffee shops continue the conversation in louder tones. More formal discussion takes place in seminars or presentations, and increasingly in events like the conversation café.

Perhaps the most productive aspect of storytelling is in the building of stronger workplace communities. Regular occasions for learning through stories, or using story to recognize the contributions of employees, is one of the best tools available to create a sense of shared values.

Story is not always benign. It may come with the best of intentions, rallying the troops to the latest change initiative. Yet this same call for help may sound suspiciously like a deliberate deceit to those who can detect the corporate spin machine sliding stealthily into action. You will hear stories pitched to defend a particular perspective, sometimes to good effect and other times sounding bombastic. Story is also the silent transmission of email slanders or the sound of whispered gossip in the hallways.

Sometimes you'll hear a harsh sound before a melody emerges as people work out their differences and misunderstandings. Your challenge is to recognize people's motives and help move them from the shadow to the light. ❧

Story with a Purpose

"No social group—whether a family, a work group, or a school group—can survive without constant informal contact among its members."

Christopher Alexander, Sara Ishikawa, Murray Silverstein. [12]

F OUR HEADS ARE HUDDLED over the table debating the case study. Across the room, there are three other groups engrossed in the same activity. The setting is institutional, a classroom in a local technical college, and everyone at this seminar is from the same company. Most have been sent by managers who reasoned their employees needed help with time management skills. There was resentment expressed at the beginning of the day about having to attend, but by three in the afternoon these employees are engaged in the content and obviously enjoying the opportunity to get to know each other better. The case studies they are solving sound suspiciously like the problems they face daily at work.

A peal of laughter indicates that someone has just caught on to the point of a story being shared by a participant at the table nearest me. Laughter is one of the by-products of storytelling. The interactive nature of the seminar has also encouraged knowledge-sharing through stories, an activity that occurs all too rarely at their place of work. Participants have complained of putting in long hours without adequate supervision, training and resources. My hope is they will take what they have learned in the seminar, especially collaborating to solve problems, and apply these skills in their workplace. The storytelling has helped draw out knowledge they already possess.

Storytelling is the glue in many workplaces, boosting morale and motivating employees. The participants in this workshop are using storytelling in a purposeful way in order to solve time management issues. What is happening is richer than mere resolution of a problem. People are connecting as they interact, trust is being strengthened, and this morning's negativity has been transformed into a sense of purpose. Ironically, these employees have told me that communications "suck" in their workplace—yet here, in the context of a non-judgmental and safe environment, they seem to excel at getting to the heart of the matter.

What does the productive use of story sound like at work? A familiar example would be one team member telling an uplifting story to encourage others. When I want to motivate a group that is despondent about a project, I tell them the story of Larry Kwong.[13]

Kwong was an entrepreneur and athlete. In his youth he was a hockey player and the first Chinese Canadian in the National Hockey League. Kwong played with the New York Rangers in the 1947-48 season. He had an illustrious career playing hockey in other leagues after that brief stint and would go on to win a national award for sportsmanship. He also played hockey in England and coached in Lausanne, Switzerland. But because of his race, Kwong only got one minute of ice time during an NHL game. His skills were never in dispute.

Larry Kwong's story is a tale of perseverance, from learning to skate using makeshift equipment because his family was poor, to overcoming the obstacles he encountered as a professional hockey player. When I tell his story, I let my listeners arrive at their own understanding of its significance. I have used this story to bolster team spirit and connect with people who feel overwhelmed by circumstances.

Sometimes, a story about a failure can be more powerful than a success story in creating a sense of connection. One of my colleagues, for example, tells a war story that became a legend for her firm. A client had asked the office to deliver training to 50 disgruntled employees, and to oblige him, one of the firm's top facilitators was flown in, as well as a second facilitator to assist with small groups. It was assumed all bases were covered until the backup accidentally bonked the lead facilitator on the head minutes before the session started. The lead was whisked away to the hospital for stitches and the backup bravely took over, but she wasn't prepared to lead the show, and the day was a catastrophe.

My colleague jokes about all the finagling required to save that client relationship, including a repeat workshop at no cost. The story was retold often—scars and all—every time staff found itself in sticky situations.

Change experts like John Kotter and Dan Cohen have demonstrated that storytelling speaks to people's feelings rather than their heads. In their bestselling book *The Heart of Change* they argue if you want to motivate employees, forget a purely rational approach and tell a story instead.

Harry Ulmer, a manager at Duke Energy® Gas Transmission in Calgary, uses stories for just this purpose. "My employees are smart," he says. "They don't need much guidance from me. My job is to communicate enthusiasm, passion and interest in their work and to demonstrate I trust them."

Most of Harry's stories are pulled from his athletic and volunteer experiences. "I might tell a story about my volunteer committee work where our job was to reach consensus in spite of our differences," he explains. "I've seen people shift apparently fixed positions in the course of deliberations. Sometimes, they actually did an about face. When I tell my team a story about one of these encounters, it's like flipping a switch. Team members think about the times they've been in adversarial relationships with customers or other departments. And then they consider what could happen if they were willing to shift from a particular position to seek a common solution instead." Harry refers to this as "solutioning" instead of "positioning".

In workplaces everywhere there are storytellers who generously share narratives to support and challenge their workmates to reach higher. These stories can take the form of sports stories like Kwong's, they can be metaphors for persevering or moving on, and sometimes they are the personal stories people share with other. A workplace without the sound of these stories would be a grim place indeed. ❧

Inspiration in the Ordinary

"The remarkable stories of most people's lives hardly ever
get told or seen as remarkable. Once you start to listen
to those stories you begin to recognize something. You
begin to see that the people you thought you knew are far
more than you ever imagined."

Warren Redman. [14]

STORY CAN SOUND REMARKABLY ORDINARY, more like a melody
hummed under the breath than a rousing Broadway production. You don't need to go to music or theatre camp to tell stories
that matter at work.

In a weekly staff session called Ordinary People, Ordinary Lives,
managers at the Developmental Disabilities Resource Centre of
Calgary (DDRC) meet to share stories. [15] These are solicited from
employees working with clients who are developmentally delayed
or disabled: people with Down Syndrome or Autism, for instance.
Some of these are success stories, affirming the agency's mandate to
promote inclusion for their client group into the wider community.
There are many naysayers who oppose the idea of inclusion, including other social service agencies engaged with a similar clientele.
By narrating these weekly tales about ordinary people with disabilities leading ordinary lives, the organization affirms its mission
and encourages its supporters.

To give you a sense of an "ordinary story", here is "Marie's":
Like many adults who were originally cared for in sheltered

situations, Marie had no experience of life in the community. She grew up at a time when people with developmental disabilities were housed in special schools and homes. When she reached adulthood, she was relocated to a sheltered workshop environment for people with disabilities. Marie would get up in the morning and be chauffeured to the workshop. At work, she was treated as someone with a disability, someone incapable of accomplishing what "normal" people do. At night, she would return to the safety of her home. Her world was very small indeed.

When DDRC chose to move away from sheltered workshops, a result of much soul searching and funding cuts, Marie was deinstitutionalized. Her family was concerned: would she be safe in a regular workplace setting, and who would look after her if she needed help? Where would she find work? Would she fit in? Like Marie, her family had been conditioned to see her as someone in need of chronic care. After assessing her interests and skills, the agency discovered Marie's passion for doing laundry. She enjoyed sorting lights from darks, selecting the correct wash cycle and folding each item as it emerged from the dryer. A job search produced the ideal position in the laundry room of a large hotel.

The family went through a period of anxiety when Marie started her new job, worrying for her safety. Staff at the hotel was wary too: how should employees interact with this special person in their midst? In a short period of time, the miracle began to happen. Marie's specialness brought out the best in employees. There was a subtle but tangible change in the environment. Watching out for Marie made them more caring for each other and the hotel guests. Marie's family discovered she had strengths they hadn't given her credit for: a good work ethic and an ability to fit in. And Marie loves her job. She has a sense of purpose previously missing from her life. She has discovered she belongs.

This story about a woman who got a job in a laundry may sound commonplace, but if an organization tells enough stories like this, it affirms its place in the world. The motto for DDRC is "everyone belongs". Not every story may be as transforming as Marie's, but each account the DDRC shares becomes a point of connection between its employees, clients, and supporters. Every story is a reminder that everyone belongs. ∞

Corporate Myths

"Whether explaining or complaining, joking or serious, the human voice is unmistakably genuine. It can't be faked. Most corporations, on the other hand, only know how to talk in the soothing, humorless monotone of the mission statement, marketing brochure, and your-call-is-important-to-us busy signal. Same old tone, same old lies."

Excerpt from *www.cluetrain.com*.

I F YOU WERE TO PIGEON-HOLE an employee in the hallway and ask for a workplace story, chances are he would look temporarily stunned. "A story? Gee, let me think." Ask this same person for an example of what the organization says about itself to convince customers to buy or employees to tow the line, he will happily furnish you with a multitude of good lines. Every employee is wise to the organization's myths.

My informants sent me examples of corporate myths in preparing this book. Here is a short list, with their annotated remarks in parentheses:

"Diversity is our greatest strength." (Senior management is mostly cranky white males. They typically hire more people like themselves, especially for jobs in management.)

"Safety is our number one focus." (Management is pressuring people to work insane hours around here and to take short cuts to meet deadlines and budgets. We're doing this on high exposure projects where a human error can be costly.)

"We encourage work/life balance." (Who can enjoy a work/life balance when you're on call one week in four and working 10-12 hour days?)

These three examples are part of a pattern found in many organizations for which leadership is largely responsible. Myths are slogans designed to motivate staff or assure shareholders. Many employees regard them as smoke screens, so much hot air from upper management. Employees believe these myths are repeated because the organization either wants to create the right impression for newcomers or is anxious to meet minimum statutory requirements. Corporate slogans can eventually damage productivity and employee loyalty as staff becomes suspicious of everything leadership has to say.

In response to these myths you will hear the stories employees tell to denigrate management. These reflect an underlying cynicism from people who feel misled and who haven't yet found their voice.

The remedy for this particular malady is two-fold in my experience: a big dose of honesty on leadership's part and more accountability from employees who have been complaining privately rather than challenging these deceits. In a labour market where skilled, experienced workers are getting harder to come by, it would make sense to be "real" with your corporate stories rather than spout meaningless bywords—especially if you want to attract smart, dedicated people. Being real means acknowledging when you have tripped up and letting staff know what you are doing to fix the situation. You could tell a story to show your good intentions.

Acknowledging your mistakes is not so far-fetched. Your story might sound like the following example sent to me by an employee of an energy company. The company was blaming external factors for a glitch at an oil refinery that was causing the fuel to fall short of specifications. The result was damage to consumer engines using the fuel.

"An operator at one of our refineries observed that a blending process was causing our fuel to be off spec and consequently damaging consumer engines. The company was busy witch hunting everyone outside itself, but the operator pointed out somewhat sheepishly that our blending operations were not functioning properly. We investigated and discovered he was right. We owned this problem. There was no other party at fault. While this created a legal exposure for the company, a senior manager at head office decided to recognize and reward the operator for identifying the problem and coming up with practical solutions."

The writer concluded: "This is almost a whistle blower situation treated fairly."

No organization can afford to have a workplace full of disaffected, disappointed employees whose voices are shrill. Leadership needs to be exemplary in its own storytelling if it wants others to follow suit. ❧

Office Scuttlebutt

"Do not go about as a talebearer among your people."

Leviticus 19:16.

A T A MEETING I ATTENDED RECENTLY, the subject of gossip came up. Was it a harmless way to pass the time or a scourge at the office? Listening to the dialogue, it seemed to me that those who gossiped regularly were intent on defending the practice as a way to build relationships and gain acceptance at work. Those of us who have been victims of gossip and ridicule were less enthusiastic.

This is the sound of gossip relayed orally in an organization: It is a manager destroying the prospects for advancement of an employee by maligning the employee to another manager. It is two colleagues huddled together at a desk, and one says to the other with great sincerity, "Thought you'd want to know this", as a prelude to sharing a story that makes another employee sound bad. A consultant sits down to coffee with a client and proceeds to defame a fellow consultant, claiming the best of intentions.

These "insider scoops" are designed to make the narrator look superior to the victim in the story. Sharing them comes from that most human of predilections, burying a bad motive beneath an apparently good one. I have been guilty myself and know the pangs of conscience that go with the realization that I have deliberately impugned a colleague's reputation. Rarely does she have the opportunity to defend herself.

Gossip has been with us a long time. Injunctions against it are almost as old as the hills—Hebrew scripture like the quote from Leviticus warned against it more than 3000 years ago, and wisdom traditions in other cultures have long been concerned with the mischievous practice of saying something behind someone's back without giving him the opportunity to explain his side of the story.

What has changed from ancient to modern times is new technology for silently spreading gossip to the four corners of the globe with the click of a mouse. What used to be mischief between a narrator and one or two listeners has become slander on a grand scale. Today, you can cut a person's reputation to shreds with a few well-aimed emails. Your message may call into question someone's competence or imply failings of a more personal nature. Taken to the extreme, gossip can become libellous and grounds for a court case.

Gossip often originates with one person who feels sore or threatened by someone else and who then buries these negative feelings beneath a veneer of superiority, claiming knowledge and understanding of the other person's motives. A third party hearing the gossip, wanting to fit in, confidently passes it on to a friend. With each telling, a new spin is put on the story making its impact increasingly harmful. If there was any substance to the original narrative, it has long since been lost.

At issue here is not whether the talebearer is telling the truth.[16] Some of what passes for gossip may be true. The difficulty is that gossip never gives us the whole picture. Even if what the gossip says about you is factual, it is not helpful to repeat it, and rarely does anyone think to ask you for your side of the story. People who gossip may even appear to be well disposed toward their victim: "We've been buddies for a long time. I thought I knew her. Never would have guessed she'd do something like this."

Regardless of the gossip's intentions, the consequences remain the same. If I take someone into my confidence with a piece of gossip, there is no guarantee my confidant won't repeat it. Unless she chooses to ignore the tale, what was a story between two people can quickly become legion. The repercussions for gossiping are widespread and long-lasting. I have no control over what my listeners do with my stories, even the ones I regret.

How do you put a halt to gossip that has run amuck at the office? One response is to challenge it directly. Research has shown that when gossip is confronted in a group situation, it quickly peters out. You can initiate new topics and change the tone of the conversation by sharing ideas or solutions to real problems in the workplace. You can also organize your workday so that you avoid gossip. Managers would be wise to avoid gossiping themselves and model open and accurate communications.

The antidote to this kind of storytelling in organizations is clear: each of us is responsible for what we say, and gossip is a sure-fire way to undermine your integrity. Guarding your tongue and examining your motives will keep you from getting a reputation as a talebearer at work. ❧

Victim Narratives

"All sorrows can be borne if you put them into a story or tell a story about them."

Isak Dinesan—Danish author.

J AKE IS AN ENTREPRENEUR whose publicly-traded company is being threatened with closure by the Stock Exchange. If you ask him why, he will tell you a story about fickle investors, greedy lawyers and venture capitalists, and his (ex) wife, all of whom he believes sabotaged the business. Listening carefully, you will hear the hurt tones of someone who feels betrayed by the people he thought he could trust.

At a financial institution down the street, Melanie is a manager who has reached the end of her tether. To hear her tell it, after introducing dozens of badly-conceived changes the company is in chaos and the change process has stalled. Melanie is convinced that too much is being asked of employees. Her response has been to badmouth senior leadership. She sounds resentful and like a saboteur herself.

Alistair completes this threesome. He is a senior account agent at an energy firm. Alistair was recently arrested for driving under the influence after a staff social. His company has a policy that mandates counselling or treatment for anyone who incurs a police record for drunk driving. Sit him down over a beer, and he'll tell you how he was hauled up in front of the manager of Human Resources. The manager wasn't remotely sympathetic and insisted Alistair attend sessions with an addictions counsellor. With a howl of outrage—or is it despair?—Alistair will describe his bi-weekly counselling session, a condition of his retaining his job. Alistair is still blaming the company for his arrest and Human Resources for the conditions that have been imposed.

These are some of the sounds of story at work. Not all storytelling sounds melodious or inspirational. Regardless of its expression, however, all story has value. None of these actors is going to make any progress without narrating their stories. They need to know they have been heard. While you may be critical of their tales, and frustrated by their inability to recognize what they are doing to themselves, only by working their way through their stories will they eventually come to an understanding of how to move on.

TRADING POWER FOR SYMPATHY

A typical victim story has a cast of three: a victim, persecutor and rescuer. Jake's persecutors are his investors, lawyers and wife; Melanie is victim to a corporate change process; Alistair's dragon is the manager in Human Resources. We're not sure yet who the rescuers are, because like most victims these three are waiting for their rescuers to appear. Jake needs a millionaire investor, Melanie might prefer a fairy godmother or prince charming from the kinder side of management, and Alistair's rescuer is probably a powerful senior manager who would release him from the probation he is under.

Psychologists tell us that when I narrate a story that casts me as a victim, much as Jake, Melanie and Alistair have done, I trade power for sympathy. Rather than choosing to be accountable for what has happened, I blame someone else or external circumstances. It appears I would rather you felt sorry for me and took my side than do the adult thing and be responsible for the predicament I'm in. There's nothing unique about this kind of response; most of us have experienced it at one time or another. Our threesome would be surprised and dismayed to be informed they have been behaving like victims.

FINDING RESOLUTION

As the manager for Melanie or Alistair, or a board director at Jake's firm, what will you do? Fire the offender for being sore? Terminating an employee eliminates the opportunity for learning and leaves you on the hook for a replacement. Work with the victim? An intimidating prospect if she is particularly strident in expressing her resentment. Certainly you want to understand and address the problem behaviour, either with professional help or by tackling it yourself.

Not only can I paint myself into a corner with storytelling, but it also offers me a way out. With direction from a skilful manager or counsellor or in a supportive peer group setting, I will have the opportunity to come to terms with my victim stance, learning to reframe my story. Perhaps I was never a victim after all, and maybe with repeated narration will come the insight that the only way to move on is to forgive myself for feeling victimized and to try to understand the motives and actions of my persecutors. Gradually I'll move from the victim's role into that of the survivor.

It turns out there are choices I can make, choices I had failed to appreciate when I felt victimized. Not only do these choices make me more accountable, but they also give me a sense of being in charge. With some time and perspective, I may even come to see that what appeared to be an insurmountable situation created by others was actually a stepping stone to greater understanding of myself.

A victim narrative is no less legitimate than the story you might tell to help a friend through a hard time. During times of personal or organizational change people often end up spending a long time in a no man's land of uncertainty. To deal with the uncertainty, they narrate stories that cast the perpetrators of the change in a glaring light. A combination of any two of the following—listening to their stories, training, coaching, counselling or mentoring—can help restore the victim to a more productive role.

Telling more stories in order to counter the adverse effects of a victim narrative is a bit like taking the hair of the dog to cure what ails you. Story can trap and wound, but another dose can also be applied for healing purposes. ✂

Heroes and Survivors

"Because the story of our life becomes our life."

Lisel Mueller. [17]

O UR SPEAKER IS A RESPECTED university professor who has devoted his life to education. His theme is a familiar one, how years of government cutbacks have undermined the ability of his faculty to deliver a superior arts and science education. The audience is composed of alumni, in most cases many years removed from academia and more anxious to find new business contacts and have fun than endure a lecture from a disappointed academic.

The presentation begins with a series of graphs demonstrating the correlation between government cutbacks and class size. We learn that over the last decade, the ratio of students to professors has been rising continuously. The professor's message is bleak. The only way to reverse this situation is by donor support for the endowment of Chairs in faculties. We are informed that to endow a Chair means a donation of at least five million dollars.

Most of us in the room are not in a position to endow anyone. We are business people earning middle class incomes with good intentions about renewing our relationship with the old Alma Mater. The presenter's gloominess has a profound effect. When I ask how our modest donations can make a difference at the undergraduate level, his response is that the best we can hope to do is buy frills. "Frills? Who wants to give money for frills?" I wonder with exasperation. This man needs a new story if he wants me to become a donor!

The professor's presentation isn't just the story of a faculty in the throes of change. This man's disappointment is keen and after ten years of struggling, he is leaving—packing it in. He has lost hope and by extension, so has his faculty. I doubt he understands the impression he has created. Sadly, he has become stuck in the victim's role, unwilling or unable to transition into that of plucky survivor.

What story are you telling about your organization or your place in it? Is your story motivating your team-mates, donors and investors or is it putting a damper on enthusiastic support for your objectives? Does your story depict you as a survivor or victim? Be careful. Your story does more than provide information or entertain. A self-limiting story can actually hold you back. As Pulitzer Prize-winning poet Lisel Mueller has remarked, "The story of our life becomes our life." How you narrate your personal or organizational story not only reflects your outlook but can have a profound influence on how you behave in the world.

Storytellers and playwrights have long recognized that by focusing on the courageous aspects of your story, you transcend the victim's status to become a survivor or hero. You become someone who takes initiative rather than being acted upon. Talk-show hosts, speakers and therapists—today's creators and interpreters of stories—frequently employ this technique. Listen to a professional speaker in presentation, or tune in any day to *Oprah* to hear people reframing their lives through story. We may sympathize with victims, but we connect with survivors.

Rather than presenting his faculty as having been victimized for more than a decade by philistines holding elected office, the professor could have narrated stories about the university's best efforts to turn around a bad situation. How we narrate an organizational story and how we see ourselves may be related. What's your personal story like?

My own story is a case in point. I grew up feeling I had been abandoned as a child, the result of my parents' bankruptcy when

I was five. It is only recently that I have begun to appreciate that during the worst fallout from this financial crisis, when neither of my parents was emotionally present, a neighbour cared for me. This neighbour's generosity could just as easily define the story of my childhood as my parents' emotional absence.

Reframing my story might change how I see myself. Rather than casting myself as a solitary, struggling entrepreneur, I could become a business woman who has triumphed over adversity and who never lacks for supportive colleagues and customers.

A survivor's story is not necessarily a "success story" in the conventional sense of money earned, goods sold or a series of successes along the way. It might be the story your team tells about negotiating with management for more resources to do your job well. Perhaps it is the tale of how you banded together to challenge a competitor. It could be your personal story of becoming more accountable. Whatever the circumstance, the sound of a survivor's tale can be jubilant, a far cry from the recriminations or sorrow of a victim.

As for the professor, he could have given a more upbeat presentation that would have engaged our hearts and wallets. Where were the stories about the social and educational impact made by previous donations? What about the faculty's innovative practices for instructing on smaller budgets or collaborating with other partners to achieve academic excellence? Or his own story of overcoming adverse circumstances to make a difference for his faculty?

Storyteller and physician Rachel Naomi Remen defines a victim as a survivor who just doesn't know it yet. As you learn to retell your personal or corporate story from the survivor or hero's standpoint, you come to see yourself in a new way. Eventually, you begin to behave differently, further altering your story and frame of reference. ❧

Summary II

1. From melodious to muffled to raucous, the sound of story is all around you in the workplace. The stories you hear are a reflection of the narrators' motives.

2. Productive stories don't have to describe successes at work. Sometimes a story about a failure is more powerful than a success story for enhancing a sense of belonging in the workplace.

3. A seemingly ordinary story can be at least as inspiring for your listeners as one set in extraordinary or dramatic circumstances.

4. There's a difference between meaningful storytelling and corporate myth-making. To maintain trust in your stories, avoid promotional narratives and be honest about your mistakes.

5. Gossip is rarely benign and is a recipe for undermining your integrity. You never know what your listener will do with your gossip.

6. Victim narratives are a legitimate form of storytelling. These stories can be an effective way for coming to terms with someone else's actions or your own mistakes.

7. Stories do more than inform or entertain. How you present yourself in a story—as victim, survivor or hero—has a profound impact on how others perceive you. Be careful how you tell your story!

Section III

Storyteller in the
Workplace

"A person is like a letter of an alphabet; to produce a word it must combine with another."

Benjamin Mandelstamm, *Mishle Binyamin.* [18]

WHO GETS TO TELL STORIES in an organization? Are some people more qualified than others? What role does a storyteller play in organizational change? What distinguishes the outlook or behaviour of a storyteller from other employees?

These are tough questions, and in the best tradition of storytelling, not always answered with direct responses. In listening to storytellers over the past 20 years, I have learned that every organization has official and unofficial storytellers. The official ones are easy to spot. They have titles—Communications Director, Public Relations Coordinator, Vice-President Sales and Marketing, and Manager, Human Resources. I would like to add another category, purely out of self-interest: Organizational Storyteller.

The unofficial storytellers actually exercise more influence than the company-sanctioned staff. Naysayers and gossips, mentors and coaches, loud mouths and heartfelt friends: this is the real cast of storytellers and they do most of the talking in an organization.

There are many textbooks on how to be an official storyteller. That's not my plan here. What you will find are directions of a sort, a map for finding your way along the dusty paths that every Real Storyteller walks in order to tell stories that matter.

In this section we'll begin by looking at your role in the organization and the potential and responsibility that carries. Benjamin Mandelstamm's quote about individual letters needing to combine in order to make words is an artful way to understand your role as storyteller. If you are going to tell stories, see yourself as a part of the larger whole, as connected to your fellows at work. We'll begin to explore the holistic mindset that every great storyteller brings to narrative. In the course of our journey together, you will discover that being a storyteller is both demanding and exhilarating. I hope you choose to persevere. ❧

Market Tales

"In the late afternoon sunlight, the storyteller takes her place in the market square. Gradually, people begin to drift her way. She asks them for their news, and listens carefully to the expression of their longing and concern. Then, she begins her story."

Andrée Iffrig, metaphor for WaveCommunications © 2006.

THIS METAPHOR ILLUSTRATES the most important principle of storytelling: if you want to tell stories at work, find out what matters to the people you work with before you craft your tale. Listening is the first step in creating meaningful stories. By accounting for your audience's concerns and hopes, you are less likely to relay a message they find irrelevant or unsympathetic.

The significance of this principle was explained to me in Indonesia by a doctor I interviewed.[19] The non-profit organization he led was the focus of a case study I was conducting. There is always a danger in writing a case study that your cultural bias will colour the narrative. My doctor friend wanted to ensure that I did not write his organization's story from a western perspective. In the best Indonesian tradition, he told me a story.

It seems there was a doctor working in the villages of Central Java. He had little experience of life in a poor village, but he had a good heart and grieved every time one of the village children died. Visiting one of the poorest villages, he was alarmed by the high child mortality rate and suggested the construction of a health post. The post was to be manned by volunteers who would educate their fellows in different aspects of primary health care. The doctor gathered the elders of the community together and explained his proposal.

To the doctor's amazement the villagers showed no interest in his plan. Again and again over the next few months he explained the reasons for the health post and promoting better hygiene, and each time was met with indifference. The villagers complained they were too busy just existing to become health volunteers. One day, having travelled to the furthest part of the village, the doctor noticed poor farmers carrying buckets of water from a great distance in order to irrigate their fields. "Why is this necessary?" he asked. The farmers explained that their land was some distance from where the largest water reserves were located; in times of drought, their only option was to hand carry what water they could to their land. "What if there was a dam and an irrigation system to transport water instead?" The farmers agreed that would be best, but how could they, poor farmers, build a dam and irrigation system?

The doctor set to work, meeting first with village elders to discuss what kind of infrastructure would be necessary to irrigate all of the village's fields. Once he understood the farmers' needs, a committee was formed and together with the committee's representatives, the doctor met with the largest landowners whose properties bordered the water reserves. A deal was struck and with help from a non-government agency, a dam and water system were built for the entire village. With construction complete, the villagers thanked the doctor and asked him what they could do to save their children. It was then that the doctor began his real work in primary health care in the villages of central Java. Today, hundreds of thousands of people benefit from his original vision.

There is a nice irony in this story. The doctor sees a need for better health care, but in his egocentricity has missed the villagers' more pressing water issue. He wants to tell them a story about hygiene and health, but they are only interested in hearing a story that reflects their agricultural concerns. Only when he has taken the trouble to see things from their perspective are they willing to see things from his. We can draw some valuable lessons from this story.

- If you want people to listen to your stories, don't make assumptions about their objectives and concerns; ask them what matters to them and tailor your narrative to their circumstances.
- It takes time to create a bond of trust with your audience—be prepared to invest considerable time in cultivating relationships in your workplace. That storyteller has been hanging out in the market square for some time.
- Learn to listen to what people say and what they do not say; "white space" in a dialogue is a sign that people are not telling you the whole story. Persevere to come to a better understanding of the real issues at play.
- Cultivate self-understanding; learn to recognize your own biases so these don't interfere with your ability to narrate meaningful stories.

Great storytellers care about their audiences. Like the storyteller in the market square, they combine a passion for dialogue and sharing ideas with a genuine interest in finding out about their listeners. Practice these principles, and you are halfway there. ❧

Storyteller—Leadership Connection

"At Nokia we got literally hundreds of people involved in imagining What Could Be: What new needs can we serve? How can we use our competencies in different ways? How can we change the economics of this industry? Out of that came hundreds of ideas, and the real work of top management was not to generate the new thinking but to look at all these ideas and try to find the fundamental themes that would give overall direction to the company."

Gary Hamel. [20]

THE SCENE IS A LITTLE SURREAL. There is jazz music playing in the background and a dramatic view of the Rockies from the window. Artists float about the room, dressed like bohemians and dripping with beads and Native Indian jewellery. The senior managers look smart but casual in their golf clothes. Along with curious consultants like me, we are dispersed at tables in a lounge at the Banff Centre for this leadership workshop. It is a warm summer evening and people look expectant as the facilitator introduces the theme for this conversation café. We have been asked a Big Question: If innovation and creativity are essential in organizations, does a leader have to be innovative herself? A secondary question arises: Do practicing artists, who are by nature creative, have anything to teach us about leadership?

The conversation is animated as leaders and artists take turns reflecting on the questions. In spite of significant lifestyle differences between the two groups, there is consensus: great leaders don't have to be innovators and creators themselves, but they do need to challenge conventional ways for getting things done in the organization. It is a leader's job to make it possible for other people to be innovative and creative. Coincidentally, artists and innovators don't have to be capable of leading, but it helps to be supportive of leadership's efforts and to behave in ethical and thoughtful ways.

Using this same principle we could say that leaders don't have to be storytellers, but they can choose to create conditions conducive to storytelling. And people who take on the mantle of sharing stories would want to behave in a manner worthy of leadership

Most organizations are dynamic at best and chaotic and dysfunctional at worst. Today's change-battered employees can be forgiven for asking: "Who are we? Where are we going? Why are we doing this?" It is a leader's job to answer questions like these, to provide vision and ensure an orderly direction so that people can accomplish their tasks. Storytelling helps tackle employee concerns, providing a window for exploring a variety of answers. And there is a bonus: sharing stories encourages the development of a reflective capacity in tellers and listeners alike.

If the leader lacks a storyteller's skills, this need not be an impediment. As Gary Hamel's quote suggests, leadership's job is to encourage ideas and innovation and to cull from them themes that can give overall direction to the company. People throughout the organization can do the actual storytelling: the more who commit to this undertaking, the better.

This brings us to the question, "Can anyone in the organization lead with stories", or, "Who qualifies?" This is tricky, because inherent within the question is the idea that some are more worthy than others. Organizations can ill afford to silence some employees in favour of others when it comes to stories of encouragement. And they seldom control who says what anyway, as untold numbers of hostile web blogs and derogatory emails indicate.

Since you can't silence the malicious storytellers, why not encourage the considerate ones? These people may not always tow the company line, but they will ask good questions and work collaboratively with others to achieve results. Innovation needs these supporters, and no change effort will succeed without their contribution.

PROFILE FOR A STORYTELLER/LEADER

What does it mean to be a storyteller who leads with stories? Do you qualify? Here is a profile for a storyteller/leader:

- You could be anywhere in the organization—rank and title have nothing to do with your ability to tell a good story, especially one that makes a difference for your colleagues or the wider organization.
- As a leader, you understand that storytelling carries a responsibility to be honest and open; ethical behaviour is a key constituent of leadership.
- Loyalty to the team or organization carries a high priority. This doesn't mean you can't challenge the team—all great leaders understand the need for being provocative—but you come from a place of being part of the team, not outside it slinging arrows.
- Respectful listening is one of your core values: great storytellers are not stage hounds. They are willing to learn from others, and they cultivate a reflective capacity.
- You recognize that others need to tell stories as well, and you encourage and support this activity. We could call this succession planning for storytellers!
- Just as leadership is a way of being and acting in the world, so you choose to lead by example with your storytelling; this is reflected in your choice of appropriate language and a positive perspective.

No leader is ever going to possess every skill or attribute ideal for the job. Most storytellers would fail the halo test, which is arguably what makes their storytelling so compelling. What counts is that your intentions are good, you care about the situation of your colleagues, and you want to contribute to the development of a sustainable organization. If you possess these characteristics, then it is high time to begin your storytelling apprenticeship. ❧

Holographic Nature of Storytelling

To see a World in a Grain of Sand
And Heaven in a Wild Flower
Hold Infinity in the palm of your hand
And Eternity in an hour

William Blake. [21]

S TEVE AND JACOB HAVE JUST FIRED us off a draft strategic plan. Preparations have been underway for several months, with six of us participating in the planning exercise. Reading this latest draft of the agency's plan, it suddenly strikes me why I have been so uncomfortable with this carefully worded and itemized document. I can't see the forest for the trees. Lost in a mass of detail about different programs and functions is what the agency will actually look like in five years when all this planning has finally come to pass.

I need to hear stories about that day in the future, not be mired in details about a particular program or some aspect of operations. Tell me about the workplace and the people who will be employed there; we are projecting 50% growth which means a move to new office space and more employees at the agency. Tell me a story about a family we are currently helping with counselling and job finding skills. How will their lives have changed?

Our Executive Director Bev will be presenting this plan to the rest of the board for approval. If she presents this document as is, board directors will become lost in the details, when what they really need is a lively synopsis of the future. Phoning Jacob, I explain my difficulty. Jacob and Steve have invested several volunteer hours into this plan, and I don't want to cause hurt feelings. The moment the words "I can't see the forest for the trees" are out of my mouth, Jacob knows exactly what I mean.

Most organizations tend to see themselves as composed of discrete functions. A common dichotomy would be financial and administrative services, operations, human resources, and the executive function. In the oil and gas sector which dominates my region, companies divide operations into "upstream" and "downstream"; further division of upstream might consist of exploration, drilling, completions, production, marketing and pipeline groups. The tasks of carrying the vision, strategizing, and acting on behalf of the whole organization, would fall to the executive management team and the board of directors.

Conceiving an organization as a collection of all these bits and pieces is the equivalent of assembling a photographic image of the human body made from a composite of body parts. Imagine photographing the heads, arms, legs and torsos of several people and then creating a single image of a human body with selections from the various shots. With practice, you might get something resembling a human form; with less art you would end up with Frankenstein. (Some of you will relate to the latter as you reflect on your own organizations).

To imagine an organization three to five years out, a holistic perspective works better than a bits-and-pieces one. Stories are ideal transmitters because storytelling is holistic by nature. It paints big pictures from the smallest of parts. This is precisely what our Executive Director needs to do for our board—to paint a picture of the agency that the rest of us can appreciate and enthusiastically support. In creating this picture she will need to draw on our detailed planning, but it is the whole that will engage people's imaginations.

HOLOGRAPHIC NATURE OF STORYTELLING

Holography, as Michael Talbot explained in his book, *The Holographic Universe* (1991), is a way of creating an image so that the whole of the image is contained in every part. A holographic image is captured by shining an array of laser beams at the image and recording the interference of these waves on a photographic plate. Displaying this interference pattern produces a three dimensional image that is projected in space.

Using the metaphor of a flower,[22] Talbot illustrated how a hologram of a rose would differ from a photograph. If you take a photograph of a rose and cut the print in half horizontally, you end up with petals in the upper half and a stem and leaves in the lower half. A rose's hologram is quite different. If you cut the image in half and then illuminate each half with a laser, each part still contains the entire image of the rose. True, the resolution has been affected—it is not quite as detailed as the original—but you can still see in each half the entire rose: petals, stems and leaves.

As Talbot pointed out, the hologram's "whole in every part" nature is an entirely different way of understanding organization and order. Instead of dissecting the organization into its constituent parts, the viewer is invited to take in the big picture. The early drafts of our strategic plan failed to communicate this bigger picture because we were too preoccupied with the individual components. By incorporating stories that paint vibrant pictures of the future, we can overcome this deficiency and still make good use of the detail we generated.

Just as the degree of resolution in a hologram is a function of its wholeness, so the power of a story is a function of the experience you bring to it. With a hologram, even though all information for the image is stored in each individual part, the whole contains more information than any one of the parts. You may be able to discern the image of the rose in each half, but its beauty is more apparent in the original whole where the resolution was at its highest. Bev's stories will be more engaging for all that detail we created in our strategic planning, and your stories will be richer for being informed by your personal experience, not just your professional knowledge.

TRANSCENDING ORGANIZATIONAL ORDER
WITH STORYTELLING

A holographic view of the universe suggests that at some deeper level of reality all things are infinitely interconnected. Scientific studies have confirmed this. Experiments with subatomic particles or electrons have shown that under certain circumstances, these miniscule bits of matter are able to instantaneously communicate with each other regardless of the distance between them. Physicists speculate this is not because the electrons are sending a mysterious signal back and forth, but because their separateness is an illusion.

If you apply the principles demonstrated by these experiments to human and organizational activity, you come to the insight that none of us is so separate after all. These experiments also help us understand why people listening to your stories experience a connection to your content: we are all made of the same "stuff" in spite of individual differences.

The idea that at some deeper level we are interconnected and part of some larger whole, suggests we share similar hopes and concerns. At its best, storytelling can help us overcome our illusion of separateness.

Story, like a grain of sand or wildflower, can explain the whole of the universe because of its universalism. Interestingly, neither the grain nor the wildflower is aware of this momentous capability. They just "are". Stories have this same inherent artfulness and possibility. And when you narrate a story by way of helping others with their struggles, you model behaviour that reflects some greater wholeness or coherence in the universe.[23]

Whether or not your story is appreciated by others is inconsequential in the grand scale of things. It will always have an inherent value—and potential—that transcends your intentions and delivery. ❧

Objective Storytelling
is an Oxymoron

"The world of reality has its limits; the world of imagination
is boundless."

Jean-Jacques Rousseau.

I F YOU ARE GOING TO STEP into the role of storyteller, whether
officially sanctioned by the organization or not, abandon the idea
of "being objective" with your stories. In every story you narrate
some of your past, your class, your phobias and self-talk will inevitably impose itself. Better to acknowledge these influences than
pretend they don't exist.

Storytellers need to work constantly at knowing themselves and
that requires being honest about your foibles and strengths. This
studied self-reflexivity is part and parcel of any personal journey as
the wanderers amongst us will tell you. To be real means showing
your hand and letting listeners in on your journey.

For years I told stories and gave presentations maintaining a
careful emotional distance from my audiences. I thought it would
be unprofessional to reveal anything about my past or how my present circumstances were affecting my outlook. I would get up in the
morning, don face paint and an expensive suit and hope nobody
would guess that underneath all those layers there was a frightened
woman pretending to be an accomplished grownup with a message. My objective was to look professional and business-like, but

I finished every story feeling like a fraud. Strangely, being business-like did not enhance my storytelling skills, and my audiences found me remote.

I suffered another handicap in my attempts to be objective. In presenting what appeared to be a body of facts, my ability to be persuasive diminished. This goes contrary to what most of us have been taught. Conventional wisdom says a professional uses facts to deliver a persuasive presentation. This may work for marketing a stock portfolio to investors, but being convincing in a story has less to do with facts than with your sincerity and connection with the audience.

It is easy to spot a storyteller who isn't real, especially in a workplace setting. He will either be too familiar for comfort or cold as yesterday's toast. You will hear the use of the royal "we" as though he were superior to others in the room. Alternatively, he may imply an intimacy with the audience, using "you", without having a genuine connection. I finally learned to be real by taking what I had observed in 12-step settings and transferring it to other storytelling venues. People speak from the heart in the rooms of the 12 steps. They share their struggles and their hopes, and rarely does anyone rehearse in advance. Humility and honesty carry a high premium as does the ability to laugh at yourself.

It has been a relief to abandon the objectivity charade in favour of a more personal approach to storytelling. In the process, I have found my voice and learned to like myself better. My audiences seem to appreciate the new me.

To enhance my own comfort with storytelling, I regularly hold storytelling gatherings in my home, and I attend a local chapter of the speaking organization, Toastmasters. These venues have provided an emotionally safe environment for trying out new stories or reworking old ones. There was a magic moment that occurred when I finally came clean about some of the personal and professional challenges I have faced in life; suddenly I connected with all the other real people in the audience. It was a revelation to discover that an honest self-assessment presented with humour and insight was better received than an impersonal, if technically competent, presentation. I look back and realize that I was only fooling myself all those years. ❧

Real Storytellers
Show Their Feelings

If I am not for me, then who is for me?
If I am just for me, then who am I?
And if not now, then when?

Hillel. [24]

THERE IS A WAR GOING ON in the Middle East between Israel and Lebanon, and "Barbara's" usual job of coordinating community relations for a Canadian cultural agency has multiplied exponentially in the last month. The agency is supporting people suffering on one side of the conflict. Financial support is being organized by Barbara's organization before being transmitted overseas. There are letters to government officials to write and public forums to be held. Barbara is torn in all directions. It has been a crazy few weeks, and now she has to deal with cranky donors like me.

"How much of my donation is actually going to the victims?" I want to know. "What is the agency going to charge for handling funds from Canadian donors?"

I can hear the exasperation in her voice as she answers. Her cool, calm and collected public relations self has checked out, and she begins to challenge my perceptions about how much the agency spends on itself and whether that amount is justified. Barbara is the official storyteller for the agency, but her current position is much more than a job. She is dedicated to the cause of the victims and promoting public understanding of their circumstances. As she shares her frustration, a little voice inside my head says, "You've felt this way before. You know what it's like to care deeply about an issue and fight for justice in the face of indifference or criticism."

Shame-faced at my selfishness, I realize that Barbara's honesty is a breath of fresh air. My own understanding of this crisis has been that of the curious observer. I am not on the ground experiencing this conflict the way she is. By taking off her public relations mask and talking about her disappointments, frustrations and heartfelt concern, Barbara has helped me understand the gravity of the situation for both parties in the conflict.

I picture Barbara in her office, her desk crowded with letters of petition, the phone ringing constantly with inquiries from would-be donors and the curious. In the last two weeks alone she has organized a major letter-writing campaign, posted 300 letters, handled media inquiries, and been in daily contact with partner organizations in the war zone. She meets regularly with community representatives and anyone who cares to drop by her office to learn more about the crisis and the agency's response. I am spell bound as she narrates this story of devotion to the cause. Her personal tale is almost as compelling as the one taking place in a distant country.

In the midst of the current crisis, Barbara is supporting a youth initiative that brings together young people in Canada who represent the various ethnic groups at war on the other side of the world. She is after lasting peace and understanding, and here I am whining about an administration fee.

I'm glad Barbara doffed her mask. Real storytellers have too important a message to convey to let public relations protocols get in the way. ❧

Mystery

"A disciple once complained, 'You tell us stories, but you never reveal their meaning to us.'
Said the master, 'How would you like it if someone offered you fruit and chewed it up before giving it you?'"

Anonymous. [25]

I AM NOT A FAN OF "HOW-TO" LITERATURE, the kind that offers a step-by-step process for putting order back in life. I do not believe that solutions to life's big problems, at home or work, are straightforward and instantaneous, and I am suspicious of people who think they have a quick fix. Stories and metaphors appeal to me partly because they remind me of life's incomprehensibility and partly because they give me license to interpret their meaning for myself. I still want some mystery in life.

Kevin Clark is a real estate salesperson and professional speaker who employs metaphors and stories to reinforce his message. He has 30 years of experience in the real estate industry and an intimate understanding of the pitfalls practitioners face in making a living. Playing with the notion of IQ or intelligence quotient, he has created an acronym, IKEIW (Information, Knowledge, Experience, Integrity and Wisdom) to explain the attributes a real estate salesperson needs to develop a sustainable practice.

Kevin pairs the acronym with the visual of an iceberg to graphically illustrate that if all practitioners bring to a client relationship is information, their financial reward will reflect this. Information, after all, is ubiquitous—the tip of the iceberg. Beneath the surface, however, lay qualities of far greater value; qualities such as Knowledge and Experience from which clients can benefit greatly. Kevin's listeners are left to draw their own conclusions about how they can acquire the necessary attributes to sustain a successful practice. His combination of the iceberg visual and an amusing play on words for the acronym make for memorable learning.

Over the years I have catalogued examples of metaphors that intrigued me. This next analogy was the theme of the book *Teaching the Elephant to Dance* by James A. Belasco, Ph.D. I first heard the metaphor from Vaughn McIntyre, the original CEO at Charity.ca, Canada's first on-line charity portal. Vaughn is an experienced business strategist in new media and Internet-based business. This is one of many stories he narrates for people and organizations that are fearful of change:

"Look at the elephant. It is the strongest animal in the jungle, able to smash big trees by simply walking over them and yet—somehow—at the circus able to be restrained by a simple anklet bracelet chained to a one inch stake in the soft ground. Must be because of a limitation of its own making, probably being trained from an early age. If only it knew!"

If only the rest of us knew! Drawing on his experience in business, Vaughn illustrates this metaphor with concrete examples of what happens when you break the anklet and cease to be a domesticated elephant any longer. I am still finding out for myself what happens with this kind of freedom.

Not everyone is as fond of mystery as I am, especially when it comes to workplace change initiatives. In the sticky in-between place during most workplace transitions, people doubt they will ever make it out of the desert. They find ambiguity difficult and long for answers: "Why are we doing this, is it really necessary, what will happen to me, when will it be over?" Leadership often feels compelled to provide logical answers and fixed timelines. This amounts to spoon-feeding employees with the wrong kind of information. It's a game plan destined to fail.

As a workplace storyteller you play a valuable role during a transition process. Stories help people deal with life's mysteries. Stories provide word pictures, not statistical reports; metaphors, not schedules. Stories by nature invite listeners to look inside for answers.

The discussion that follows a story encourages people to grapple with what the change means. Struggling together can lead to discovery and the joint acknowledgement that it is time to move on. When you work through a process of reflection, discussion and discovery with your workmates, you end up owning the answers together.

No one wants chewed-up fruit. A little mystery via a story will pique interest and ensure ongoing dialogue about the organization's changing direction. Dialogue builds stronger organizations and more engaged employees. That's a valuable result to have achieved with your story. ❧

Summary III

1. There are designated and unofficial storytellers in any organization. The unofficial ones are usually more influential.

2. Listen carefully to the concerns and hopes of your audience. Their answers will provide you with clues about what matters to them. You can then use this information to craft meaningful stories.

3. Anyone in the organization can take on the role of storyteller. If you decide to do so, remember the position brings responsibilities as well as privileges. Act like a leader and use stories to enhance the reflective capacity of your listeners.

4. Storytelling is holistic by nature and is ideal for painting pictures of the organization's future. Every time you narrate a story, you reflect some greater wholeness in the universe.

5. "Know thyself" is one of the ground rules for storytellers. You are more likely to be persuasive if you are authentic with your listeners.

6. Real storytellers show their feelings; don't be afraid to honestly speak to your convictions.

7. Stories help people deal with life's mystery. Metaphor is an effective way to convey the unknowns in a change situation.

Section IV

Leading with Stories

"A community is like a ship; everyone ought to be prepared to take the helm."

Henrik Ibsen, Norwegian playwright.

H OW DO YOU LEAD with stories?" is one of those queries for which there are multiple answers. It begs such questions as: What does it mean to be a leader who tells stories? How would we recognize someone who was actually leading with stories? Will this person be standing on soapbox or a dais, announcing, "And now I'm going to tell a story?"

The quote from Ibsen captures the idea that organizations are stronger when the rank and file contributes. Robert W. Terry, who studied and taught leadership for many years,[26] believed that leadership involves courage, the kind that makes it possible for people to challenge unjust systems or behaviour. It requires vision, the ability to see the bigger picture that lies ahead for the organization, instead of being caught up in day-to-day particulars. Leadership is intimately bound up with ethical behaviour and integrity; employees and other supporters of the organization can hardly be expected to be enthusiastic about a leader who says one thing and does another.

In my own studies of leadership I have been impressed by the example of people who are self-aware and constantly questioning their own understanding of what it means to lead. They aren't necessarily leaders with big profiles, but they are determined and persistent as the stories that follow demonstrate. They consistently put the well-being of their fellows and the organization ahead of their own ambitions. This is not to say they are not ambitious, but they use their considerable energy and contacts to further wider organizational goals. Often they do so with little support from their higher-ups, and sometimes they actively challenge the status quo. Without exception they are change agents, and their organizations have been richer for their contributions.

The leaders in this section come from all walks of life. Some are big "L" leaders with business cards that say "Executive Director" or its equivalent, and others are blue-collar supervisors; there are the highly educated and the experienced-in-life. Regardless of their social or professional status, they mobilize people and resources to make a difference to their organizations and communities, and they do all this while telling stories. ❧

Moral Gyroscope

"The kinds of leaders that I would want to follow are the ones who do have some kind of moral gyroscope in them, which keeps them pointing in the right direction. And who tend to know basically what's right and what's wrong and don't lose sight of it in other priorities. The trouble is that quite often when we walk into the company offices, we put on another suit of clothes. We leave our real selves behind and we act a part. And that changes our priorities and our value systems."

Charles Handy. [27]

THE SETTING FOR OUR ENCOUNTER is an internet café, a fitting place to be meeting a man who owns an internet marketing company. Jeff has "entrepreneur" stamped all over him, from an energetic description of his latest business idea to his unmistakable enthusiasm for storytelling. Standing in line to order my coffee and Jeff's fruit smoothee, I wonder: What kind of story will an ambitious businessman have for me today?

Jeff already knows what he wants to talk about—ethics. He sees ethics as a provocative topic that is central to business. "Who doesn't have a story to tell about integrity in the business world?" he asks as we begin the conversation. There is the moral dilemma of whether to feed the parking meter when dashing into the bank to make a deposit (You could say to yourself, "It will only take five minutes, and who's going to know?"). Or the case of the broken ink jet printer. When Jeff called the manufacturer about a minor repair, Dell sent a new printer; meanwhile, Jeff still had the old one. Would anyone really have cared if Jeff's office had kept both printers instead of sending one back?

Jeff cites his mentor Dick Haskayne, a legendary oil man and philanthropist in Alberta, as an example of ethical leadership. Jeff tells me that Haskayne is a living example of integrity. Integrity means you are honest and ethical about even the smallest decisions because small decisions are reflective of big ones. You report the extra printer to the manufacturer because you're going to do business with it again. There are lots of opportunities to cheat in business, and it is easy to cut corners, but inevitably you will be found out, and it will affect your reputation and that of your company.

Jeff regards being ethical about the small stuff as easy. Where it becomes tricky is in the bigger things, like how you hire and fire staff. He is candid about his own mistakes and dilemmas. There was the single-parent contractor he recently hired for a client project. Jeff had his doubts about the contractor's suitability for the job, but hoped her experience and need for work would compensate for shortcomings. He was wrong: the client complained about the contractor's quality of work. Jeff had no other projects to which he could have seconded the contractor, and he was disappointed with her showing as well. He also knew that in firing this person a whole family would be affected.

The management experts may say "Hire slowly, fire fast" but in Jeff's experience it's tough to fire, period. Being ethical is rarely clear-cut. Eventually, Jeff did decide to replace the contractor with another project manager who could be relied upon, but it was a difficult call.

By sharing his struggles around ethical decision making with me, Jeff has just demonstrated two characteristics of leading with stories.

- To narrate stories with integrity means constantly questioning your motives and actions. Not just rigorous honesty but absolute vigilance is called for in telling a story.

• You have to know and understand the people whom you lead and the context in which you operate your business. This requires emotional intelligence and a big picture perspective of your industry.

Jeff has taken what could be a boring topic—ethics in business and life—and made it dynamic. I can see the parking meter at zero waiting for Jeff to feed it, and I can picture him feeling torn over firing the inept contractor raising kids on her own. Mixed in with his stories about ethical dilemmas are his reflections on people who have inspired him. His father, for one, a doctor who practiced in Africa, is the source of memorable stories that sustain Jeff in his entrepreneurial pursuits. Dick Haskayne for another. Their stories provide a moral gyroscope of sorts, ensuring that Jeff is pointed in the right direction. ❧

Small "l" Leadership,
Big "R" Results

"But what do these small, unglamorous, everyday efforts add up to? The answer is that they are almost everything. The vast majority of difficult, important human problems—both inside and outside organizations—are not solved by a swift, decisive stroke from someone at the top. What usually matters are careful, thoughtful, practical efforts by people working far from the limelight. In short, quiet leadership is what moves and changes the world."

Joseph L. Badaracco. [28]

L ET ME INTRODUCE YOU to one of those hardworking, quiet leaders who may never make the cover of a national magazine. She has come up through the ranks and struggled for credibility in organizations that frequently failed to appreciate her strengths, but that experience, combined with her own sense of fairness, has made her a leader in every workplace she has been employed. It is a role she assumed long before management thought to give it to her officially.

Susan's favourite expression is, "It is what it is". If the client is being fussy, it is what it is. If another contractor involved in a project hoards information or places impediments in her path, it is what it is. Susan doesn't play the blame game, and this has endeared her to employees. They know they can come to her with a difficulty, and she will work with them to resolve it, refraining from judging their behaviour or finding someone else to criticize. She makes them part of the solution, ensuring that every mistake is an opportunity for learning and for owning innate strengths that may have been overlooked.

Susan's company had a troublesome multi-million dollar IT project which had been abandoned by a series of project managers. After being assigned the project, she quickly realized why. She found herself dealing with a more senior contracting partner that lacked integrity. It would blame Susan's team for failure to deliver on stages of the project, yet it was withholding information her team needed, or was falling behind itself. Distraught employees would come to Susan, conscious that they could not complete their work because of the other contractor's actions. With an equanimity that most leaders would envy, Susan would invite the employee to participate in a client conference call. Together they would narrate a story for the client about the current impasse without condemning the other contractor—'it is what it is'—and find a solution satisfactory to the client. The client caught on to the source of the difficulties, and employees came to recognize that Susan was fair and supportive of their efforts.

Building relationships is a key factor in Susan's success. Rather than relying exclusively on email to contact colleagues and clients, she picks up the phone. A quick phone call makes for more immediacy than an impersonal email and ensures she gets answers and information in a timely way. She ribs employees who work down the hall from each other about their email communication. Cultivating relationships through face-to-face encounters or via phone calls gives Susan a better sense of what is going on. It also means that people tell her stories.

An accomplished storyteller, Susan is also a good listener, making her privy to stories that other managers might never hear. People tell Susan "stuff". She listens to their accounts, a little amazed sometimes at the intimacy of the sharing and mindful that it is a privilege to be a party to the conversation. She follows a communications principle emphasized by psychologist Carl Rogers who suggested that an effective listener understands from the speaker's point of view. Rogers had a rule: don't speak up for yourself until you have been able to restate the ideas and feelings of the person who spoke before you. Susan studied communication at university so she understands the theory behind effective communication, but it is her perspective on people that makes a difference.

Referring to herself as a road warrior, Susan's work has taken her to major centers in Canada and the United States. She always knew there were differences between Americans and Canadians to be accounted for during a project, but has been fascinated to discover regional differences within her own country. Work ethic does vary, with employees in some regions more willing to roll up their sleeves and put in overtime than staff in other areas. Her attitude is that everyone comes to the team with something to offer, and it is her job to find it and ensure the employee uses that strength on behalf of the project team. To that end, Susan shares meals with her employees, getting to know them and listening to their stories.

One of her work stints took Susan to Montreal. She is a died-in-the-wool Albertan; easterners refer to Albertans as rednecks because of the conservative social views that many Albertans hold. One of the members of the team was a French Canadian woman who was gay. To keep costs down on the project, the two bunked together. Susan, a mother of two, listened to her roommate's stories of an abusive childhood and the adversity she had encountered as a gay woman. Listening to these tales and others like them over the years has changed something inside Susan, making her more open and accepting of the differences between people.

Susan is no pushover—she knows when to stand up for her staff and when she is being bullied or abused. Over the years, she has learned to position her teams for success by working around difficult people and situations. Her focus on solutions rather than problems, together with her highly developed communication skills, place Susan in that rare group of people we call leaders. Like other quiet leaders she is moving and changing the world one roadblock at a time. ❧

A Rare Passion

"They have to have a dream in their mind and a fire in their belly and, in a sense, love in their heart for the people who are with them."

Charles Handy. [29]

I T IS SUNDAY MORNING, and I am listening to the animated conversation of a group of grandmothers talking about what it is like to raise children in countries devastated by HIV/AIDS. First one, then another, they have been sharing stories on CBC radio about a disease that has left millions of children orphaned in sub-Saharan Africa. A generation of adults has been felled by the disease, leaving only the children's grandmothers to raise them.

In a separate conversation with a *Globe and Mail* reporter, one of the African grandmothers describes the magnitude of her loss: her own children have died of HIV/AIDS and her one grandchild has gone to another village to live with the other grandmother. What keeps her strong is sharing her story and caring for orphaned children in her own village. [30]

Thanks to the Stephen Lewis Foundation and its donors, 100 of these African grandmothers and 200 Canadian ones are gathered in Toronto for the International AIDS Conference. The Canadian grandmothers have pledged to take back their African sisters' stories to communities all over Canada so that much needed aid can be raised to help these grandmother-led families in Africa.

Leadership for the "Grandmothers to Grandmothers" campaign comes from Stephen Lewis, who has served as the Secretary-General's Special Envoy on HIV/AIDS at the United Nations. Lewis has demonstrated a rare passion for his work and earned a reputation for being a formidable challenger of governments, institutions and corporations that have failed to carry through on promises to arrest the pandemic. This international conference means that his challenges will be front-page news for a full week, a long time in media-speak.

Every organization serious about its commitment to its employees, clients, suppliers and community needs leaders who challenge the "way we've always done things". It may be discomfiting to be confronted about our attitudes or inaction, but a leader who comes from a place of conviction, and who has vision, can convince even the most reluctant. Stephen Lewis is one such leader, and the way he goes about his work is instructive to the small "l" leader in an organization.

Lewis tells stories. At the start of his presentations, you find yourself standing with him in a village square somewhere in Africa, a witness to tragedy mixed with hope. He narrates stories about those who have been forgotten, he lashes out at the injustice of governments that have failed to produce necessary aid dollars to help the sick and impoverished, and he reminds us that this pandemic has a very human face. When he describes what it is like to have an orphan anxious for a hug clutch his pant leg, you are enveloped by the story.

Lewis has repeatedly taken on national governments, citing their failures to follow through on funding and sharply criticizing their lack of vision and leadership. In his speeches and books, he has questioned the reluctance of some African leaders to deal with the pandemic and shamed western governments and pharmaceutical companies into providing life-sustaining medication at prices impoverished African nations can afford. Nothing is sacred in his quest to find support for a continent besieged by HIV/AIDS. Whether you agree with him or not, you know he comes from a place of deep commitment and compassion for the people affected by the tragedy unfolding in Africa.

Your organization may not be engaged in life-and-death work, but if it has a conscience, and if you are the face of that conscience, stories are a way for you to challenge complacency or indifference. Just as Lewis tells stories to help western listeners understand the extent of the pandemic and its effects in Africa, so you can tell stories that remind staff that all is not well in the organization or for the clients you serve. Use stories to help people imagine a better way of getting things done. Wherever possible, give your listeners the opportunity to step into the story and connect with the experience you are trying to describe.

Many small "l" leaders with a passion for pursuing justice and making things right are quietly working away within organizations. They do not have big profiles or get featured on the front page of the newspaper. They are far-sighted and fair-minded, and they work doggedly to change their workplace environments.

One of my colleagues was asked to help a department in the civic administration address some low scores on its annual engagement survey. The department's results identified problem areas in terms of unsatisfactory communication, ongoing conflicts, and lack of respect between different employee groups. A newly appointed leader with a reputation for being a consummate team player, leader and volunteer suspected these scores were an indicator of more serious problems. When additional negative feedback cropped up in customer satisfaction surveys, she decided some kind of management intervention was required.

This leader arranged for my colleague, an organizational consultant, to interview every single employee one-on-one, giving each a chance to share her story and perceptions about the workplace. This meant that voices that were rarely heard were finally acknowledged.

The interview response rate was unusually high—96% —suggesting an elevated interest among employees in the process for improving the department's performance and environment.

In the course of the interviews, many people expressed appreciation for their co-workers' talents and qualifications, but they were also frank about conflicts and the lack of trust that undermined people's ability to work across divisions. There was a pervasive feeling, not identified in the original engagement survey, that some people worked harder than others without adequate recognition or rewards. Long-simmering resentments were making "collaboration" and "respect" mere bywords.

The effect of giving everyone a voice was electrifying. If this new leader was willing to have everyone interviewed and consider each and every concern, there might yet be hope. With the results of the stories in, the leader and her management team acted on their promises of change by meeting regularly to discuss improvements to operations. Staff had suggested the executive team lacked adequate leadership skills, and this was rectified with training and ongoing coaching—more occasions for sharing stories of challenges and learning how to surmount them.

As conditions improved, I was brought in to design a custom engagement survey. Administered annually, this survey tracks key staff concern areas and has shown a steady upward trend. Dozens of stories and three years later, a department that was at loggerheads is functioning more smoothly. Giving everyone a chance to tell their story was a key component in creating a more engaged workplace. ❧

Challenging a Corporate Myth

"In the corporate world, there is often a division between employees who directly generate revenue and those who don't. The latter are often referred to as 'overhead' or worse, 'burden' and often it feels like this group are second-class citizens. This kind of stereotyping can be damaging to people's ability to work together and undermines respect for the unique contribution each person makes in his or her own way."

Shona Welsh. [31]

COLLEEN IS A WOMAN with a mission. A corporate communications specialist, Colleen and I worked together on an initiative designed to take the pulse of a rapidly growing company. The senior leader in Canada wanted to know if newcomers were buying into the company's family culture. Was everyone aware of efforts to capture how they accomplished their jobs and shared best practices? Had their managers adequately explained career advancement opportunities?

Investigating these questions, we learned that as the company grew, the division between sales and the rest of the organization was proving an impediment to innovation and collaboration. Administrative staff and employees in the company's manufacturing and technical facilities felt their work was undervalued. Rewards and recognition flowed to the sales staff, who in turn were often critical of the work habits and outlook of other employees.

To address these misunderstandings, Colleen sought an expanded role for internal communications. I collaborated with her on the collection of stories from a good cross-section of field offices and departments. We were aiming for stories that answered the CEO's questions and illustrated how ordinary people solved the challenges they faced. What we found were a range of creative solutions delivered with integrity.

Sharing stories of their successes put each of the interviewees in a positive light and reinforced support for the company's values. It became glaringly apparent to us that most of the accolades and company perks went to those working directly on sales accounts with major corporate clients. Colleen set out to champion the cause of each and every department by publishing the stories we had collected and researching others on her own. These were heartwarming tales of getting it right for the customer, collaborating to realize organizational goals, and contributing to the communities where they work. Colleen's articles gave people a voice.

Month by month, Colleen has published these stories in the company's newsletter. Readers cannot help but observe that employees in accounting, human resources and the manufacturing plant all perform crucial work on behalf of customers. As a result of our fact-finding mission, senior leadership realized that attendance at regional gatherings and opportunities for training and development needed to be extended to the whole organization.

The newsletter continues to provide a window into daily life in every aspect of the company, and to create support and respect for each position and department. With rapid growth in the company's workforce, this kind of bonding keeps a dispersed and diverse group of people working together as a family. Stories remind people about the values they share when it comes to their families and community, values they carry over into their work for the company. Colleen's newsletter is a more sophisticated publication than when she started, but its heart is still in the same place proving that stories can and do create an understanding not easily found through other means. ❧

Basic Building Blocks

"It didn't take a genius to see why productivity was so low.
The company treated the raw material piled in the yard
better than it treated the workers."

Ken Blanchard and Stanley Bowles. [32]

THIS IS THE TEAM no one expected much of. After all, they're
just plant workers, not white collar workers at the head office.
If you work at the plant, all you have to do is put product in boxes
and move it around—right?

The team doesn't see themselves this way at all. Sure, they know
they're on the bottom of the totem pole, but sometimes being an
underdog makes you work harder to prove the naysayers wrong.

First their manager, Gary, had someone from human resources
come over and conduct a survey. She asked questions and listened
to the group's stories of feeling de-motivated about their jobs. Gary
and she collaborated on a new schedule that introduced job rotation so that everyone at the plant became responsible for learning
six jobs, not just one. At that stage they were just a mix of individuals working in close proximity, not a team, but hearing each other's
stories had the effect of creating a bond.

Once Gary had the job rotation schedule ticking along, he
decided to learn more about teambuilding. As a plant supervisor, he
hadn't rated a teambuilding course, but he asked his senior manager
for advice and got it in the form of "Gung Ho", a book by Ken
Blanchard and Sheldon Bowles. With a conviction born partly of

frustration with the wider company and partly out of a desire to make his employees more effective, he set to work building a team.

To create a foundation for a teambuilding effort, Gary held performance reviews with staff and clarified expectations for the coming year. Employees got a chance to talk about what mattered to them and to connect their career aspirations with the company's goals. Every performance interview was an opportunity to tell stories about employee concerns and to express hopes for the future.

Gary holds a weekly production meeting for his staff. It is a time for sharing his plant targets for the next few weeks, explaining how these feed into wider goals, and inviting discussion on how the team can most effectively realize these organizational objectives. There are stories that illustrate the plant's dedicated adherence to safety procedures and other tales of collaboration between team members and across departments. Meetings are also occasions for the plant's operators to identify their career goals and ways to achieve these.

Explaining the company's knowledge management initiative provided Gary with a challenge. Plant employees had been conditioned by the rest of the organization to see their jobs as insignificant. They wondered, "Why bother to map our competencies if they aren't important?" Gary held a series of educational meetings, preparing workers for the mapping process and helping them to understand how they could contribute to the theme of "better becoming best." A consultant who interviewed Gary's employees was amazed to discover they understood the initiative better than almost anyone else in the company, and their contributions were exemplary. Gary used those initial meetings to enhance their understanding of other jobs within the company they could train for.

Gary gives presentations on the plant's operations to other parts of the organization in an effort to foster understanding of the plant's processes and constraints. Stories help his listeners get a sense of the work ethic and camaraderie that characterizes employee relations in his group.

He isn't convinced his listeners are entirely sympathetic, but they seem to remember stories better than bald facts about how much product was moved last month at the warehouse facility. His goal is to correct what he regards as misplaced expectations from other departments, and to show how the plant contributes to the company's well-being. His team-mates admire his tenacity, and they know he values their efforts.

In the end, it hardly matters whether anyone else in the company endorses the team's efforts. They know their own story, and they're proud of it. ∞

Cautionary Tales

"Honesty is indivisible."

12 step wisdom.

THE PAYOFF FOR BEING HONEST in the workplace is not always clear. If you didn't plug the parking meter while racing into the bank for a five-minute visit, would it matter in the grand scale of things? If you take credit for another employee's idea, what difference will it make, especially if the employee doesn't find out? For some readers, the answer is readily apparent: honesty is indivisible. If you cheat on the small stuff you will lose sight of what constitutes honest behaviour on the big stuff. As a workgroup leader, how do you speak about the issue of integrity without sounding like a finger-wagging school teacher? The answer: tell a story.

When I was young my moral landscape was reinforced with tales like "Never Cry Wolf" and other fables. These cautionary tales illustrated the consequences for foolish or destructive behaviour. There are workplace equivalents that provide direction without preaching.

One of my favourite stories about integrity comes from Ernest Kurtz. Kurtz is a writer and storyteller with a background in addictions treatment. In *The Spirituality of Imperfection: Storytelling and the Search for Meaning*, he relates a story recounted to him during a workshop he held some years ago for social workers. They worked at an alcoholism treatment centre in the suburbs of Chicago. En route to work each morning, they took a toll road. The state highway department decided to institute an honour system on the highway, which meant that travellers no longer had to stop at a supervised toll booth. Instead they were invited to toss their coins into a basket at an unattended booth. Some of the counsellors on staff were honest and paid up every time, and others drove right through without paying the toll. "Who's going to know the difference?" was their attitude.

In a short time, the counsellors began to notice a trend at the treatment center. There were significant differences in recovery rates for patients depending on who their counsellor was. If your counsellor paid up at the toll booth on the honour system, you were more likely to get well during treatment for your addiction. If your counsellor thumbed his nose at the honour system, you were more likely to fall back into addiction. The employees who were paying up believed that to pass on the gift of sobriety from counsellor to patient required an "honest program" as a counsellor. But how could you have an honest program if you weren't fundamentally honest yourself? Honesty is indivisible.[33]

Considering the stakes involved for many addicts, a failure to get well during treatment could be a death sentence. Most workplace situations of dishonesty are not life-threatening, but they can be life changing as anyone who has ever been betrayed or abused will tell you.

Employees share their own versions of cautionary tales. One might warn another not to challenge a particular manager or "the system" for fear of repercussions. This is a kind of "Don't fall on your sword" story, often intended to discourage standing up for what you believe in. Two consultants might swap stories about a client they have in common, with the subtext, "Don't waste your time, he'll only take your information and run." A manager might narrate a cautionary tale to promote safety procedures at work. The story will be a grisly one about an employee who was grievously injured by failing to observe safety rules.

Business literature is replete these days with stories of corporations that behaved unethically. From spying on a competitor's internal website to inflating earnings reports, some corporate leaders have made a mockery of ethics. Conveying the importance of honesty and integrity in the workplace is a hard slog if you do it with Ethics 101. Stories offer an attractive alternative. The only caveat is that the storyteller must be integral as well. ◈

Summary IV

1. Storytellers with integrity constantly challenge their personal motives and actions, whether in narrating stories or while conducting business.

2. Practice the Carl Rogers' communications rule: Don't speak up for yourself until you have been able to restate the ideas and feelings of the person who spoke before you, and done it to that speaker's satisfaction.

3. As a leader in your organization, use stories to challenge conventional attitudes and behaviours that reinforce injustices or keep people from changing to meet new demands.

4. Stories are productive for acknowledging those who have been passed over in an organization and whose contributions have not been recognized.

5. Be prepared to facilitate giving everyone a chance to tell her story. Telling stories helps employees find their voice.

6. Leaders can use storytelling to convey the work ethic and performance of their employees, and to defend them against criticism from other parts of the organization.

7. With storytelling, you can provide direction for employees without preaching or teaching. Cautionary tales warn listeners about potentially dangerous or thoughtless conduct without singling out individuals for criticism.

Section v

Creating Stories

"There is no such thing as a person that nothing has happened to, and each person's story is as different as his fingertips."

Elsa Lanchester—American actress.

N OT SO LONG AGO, I would have been hard pressed to narrate my own stories. I was a consumer of stories, not a creator. Like a lot of people living in western society, I thought storytellers had to be specially trained for their role.

All the while, I was improvising stories without realizing it. Every time I attended a 12 step meeting, I told a story about my life, about the people, places, things and situations in it. These stories didn't cast me in the most flattering light; I seem to have had the greatest difficulty accepting life on life's terms, and it makes for humorous anecdotes at best and tears at my most frustrated. Nonetheless, I narrated stories at the meetings and no matter how torn or confused I was, my listeners seemed appreciative. I could see the connections in the room as I spoke.

A colleague of mine says it's not that we've lost the ability to tell stories; it is that we don't have the courage. We are not exercising our voice. We have been upstaged by higher production values, by the prettiness and slickness of the stories that are manufactured for us. I hope that you have discovered by now that real stories are not like the manufactured kind you are accustomed to at the movies, on TV and in other media.

In this section, we will explore how a persuasive story comes together and a simple way for accomplishing this, a wisdom story. It's time to create a front row seat for that audience of yours. Read on to find out how. ✺

Organic Nature of Storytelling

"The stories that sustain a spirituality of imperfection are wisdom stories. They follow a temporal format, describing "what we used to be like, what happened, and what we are like now." Such stories, however, can also do more: The sequential format makes it possible for other people's stories to become a part of 'my' story. Sometimes, for example, hearing another's story can occasion profound change. Telling the story of that change then follows the format of telling a story within *my* story: *'Once upon a time, I did not understand this very well; but then I heard this story, and now I understand very differently.'*"

Ernest Kurtz and Katherine Ketcham. [34]

H OW MANY TIMES have you sat through someone's story of a professional or life challenge and suddenly felt as though your story was being told? The details might differ but there's a sequencing that draws you in and situates you in the middle of the narrative. Rarely is there a "happy ever after" ending, but in connecting with the speaker, you feel inspired to carry on.

In the vignette, "Real Stories from Real Managers," (Section I), you met Arne. He's struggling with a sales representative who isn't following the rules for completing his monthly reports. As Arne explains the dilemma and his efforts to resolve it, he leads you through a particular sequence: from frustration at not knowing what to do about the sales rep, to asking for help from his staff, to finding an interim solution. We don't know if the recalcitrant employee ever sorts himself out, but the rest of Arne's team certainly benefits.

Arne's story is repeated over and over again in the workplace: there's a problem one person can't solve alone and cross-functional teamwork facilitates a solution. Hearing stories like these has taught me not only what makes some companies more successful than others, but how stories come together. Without a deliberate or self-conscious effort, a structure emerges in the teller's narrative. We go from how it was (the friction between Arne and the sales rep), to what happened (Arne's acknowledgement he couldn't solve the situation alone and his request for help), to what it's like now (the sales rep is making progress and the office has pulled together to help him keep his job).

Interestingly, the conclusion to the story is not always "conclusive"—not every story has all the loose ends resolved—but right here and now is at least a jumping-off point for reflection, discussion and further discovery.

Stories that follow a temporal format, describing "what it was like, what happened, and what it's like now", are called wisdom stories. People have been telling these since the dawn of civilization. All you need to narrate a wisdom story is an honest self-assessment, some experience in life and an involvement in the topic.

Over the years I have heard thousands of wisdom stories, often from people who lacked formal educations but who were rigorously honest with themselves. A wisdom story illustrates how the narrator went from one human condition to another, gaining wisdom in the passage. We can all relate to having problems, exploring answers, and gradually arriving at solutions, even if they are temporary ones. "Progress, not perfection", is a good way to sum up a wisdom story.

Sometimes, hearing another's story can lead to profound change. Ernest Kurtz and Katherine Ketcham point out that as the narrator shares her tale, you experience an "a-ha" moment. Mentally, a little voice inside your head says to you: "Wow, I've never understood it that way before. That changes everything."

In a business setting, a wisdom story might demonstrate how a mistake or painful situation was transformed into one of progress and sometimes success. You could share some information about a business problem, explain what happened to produce an improvement, and wrap up with what it's like now. You could also refer to another organization that went through a major change and came out the other end, a little wiser for coming to terms with its weaknesses and for owning its strengths.

Here is an example of organic storytelling from my work in Indonesia. When I first arrived, I was seconded to the faculty of Environmental Design at the Institute of Technology in Bandung (ITB). I spoke no Indonesian at that stage, but I was keen to become involved in community development work. I am ashamed to say I rocked up on the doorstep of the department head, Dr. Hasan Purbo, with an arrogant attitude: I was a well-educated westerner who expected a plum assignment. To my surprise, I was relegated to work on a project for garbage pickers, designing a low-tech recycling depot for the scavengers of Bandung. This seemed like a come-down from my lofty consulting ambitions. It was the best kind of humbling experience, bringing me into contact with bright students at the faculty and familiarizing me with Javanese social customs. In the course of my work, I heard this story about the origins of the project.

ITB, together with a Dutch university partner, had decided to help the garbage pickers as part of a grass roots development project. The scavengers were the poorest of the poor, living at the city's garbage dump—a foul cesspool of rotting material and disease. Entire families resided there. The academic partners planned to relocate the community and improve environmental conditions. This well-meaning exercise had almost ground to a halt, the social scientists and environmentalists having presupposed the destitute scavengers would want to relocate. They assumed wrongly: the scavengers were fearful their only source of income would disappear. Hygiene was not high on their priority list. To the chagrin of the researchers, the scavengers refused to move.

In an artful turn of events, students at ITB got around the difficulties created by the Wise Adults. The students had noticed that the scavenger couples were unmarried; inquiring, they learned these homeless people had neither citizenship papers nor the money to procure these. You cannot get married without papers in Indonesia. The students set to work, collaborating with the scavengers and local authorities to secure the appropriate documents. With support from local businesses, the students hosted a memorable wedding party for all of the unmarried couples in the scavenger community. In gratitude, and with their faith in the project assured, the community agreed to the relocation.

The story of the students and my own coming to terms are both examples of wisdom narratives: I went from a state of ignorance to one of greater enlightenment and acceptance. This same experience is mirrored by the change in attitude of the social scientists and environmentalists involved in the scavenging project. These narratives reinforce my conviction that even if leaders—the Wise Adults—in your organization aren't interested in supporting community building or storytelling, you can still choose to influence and motivate your team with stories. Perhaps by taking this initiative, management will take notice and investigate the benefits of storytelling.

Just as smart organizations make it possible for people at every level to contribute to solutions and practice leadership, so, too, storytelling can be widely practiced. All it takes are occasions for sharing stories and sympathetic circumstances that make it safe. I suspect that if people don't tell stories like they used to, an absence of time is only part of the problem. The other part of the equation is an environment that is hospitable to storytelling. We turn to the creation of that setting next. ❧

Storytelling Rituals

"Each person's life is a story that is telling itself in the living."

William Bridges. [35]

PICTURE A CROWDED and somewhat dingy office in Jakarta, smoke from Kretek cigarettes hanging in the air, the blades of a dusty fan wafting overhead but barely cutting the heat in the room. I am the newcomer, unfamiliar with the niceties of Javanese culture. I have been behaving like a bull in china shop by local standards. Just for today's meeting, I am determined to keep my opinions to myself and watch what other people do. Perhaps listening will reduce my agitation about trying to fit in with this group of community activists, a room full of Muslim men.

The meeting starts late, timeliness being a virtue holding little merit for the Javanese. What counts are ritual and social protocol. The most senior person in the room finally begins the meeting, introducing the guest speaker or storyteller. I watch as people ease into the story. Javanese etiquette requires that we listen without interrupting, no matter how long-winded the narrator is. Deference to rank and being personally self-contained are all-important qualities among the Javanese.

There is a pattern to storytelling that encourages sharing stories and makes it safe to do so. In the Javanese setting, a welcoming environment is manifested in a variety of ways. The narrator knows that he may tell his story without fear of being interrupted. The audience listens generously even if they do not necessarily agree with what is being said. There is an understanding that the meeting will accommodate storytelling. Protocol demands that the guest speak first, but everyone knows that over the course of the meeting, others will have a turn.

With minor changes to account for differences in culture, these rituals could be used in the average workplace in the West. Generous listening is obviously a key; the speaker needs to know she will not be constantly interrupted or judged as she tells her story. There is no right or wrong to the story—it just is what it is for her, right now. And unless time constraints prohibit this, everyone in the room has the right to share. People know what to expect. Ritual helps listeners relax and enjoy the story, rather than rehearsing a response while the story is told.

One way to create this kind of inviting environment is by establishing "terms of engagement" with your work mates. When I lead teams, I invite everyone on the team to develop these terms. They become the ground rules by which we agree to abide. Going around the table, I ask everyone to describe what a welcoming team environment would feel like. People often accompany their answers with a personal story. The team owns the guidelines it identifies at these early meetings. The terms created for a team could apply equally to promoting storytelling in organizations.

Here is a short list of ideas to consider for your own workplace:
- People need to know they will be heard, not constantly interrupted by others. Cell phones and other electronic devices are silent, and when the storyteller has centre stage, the rest of the group listens.
- Participants do not multi-task: we are focused on the task at hand.
- We agree to respect differences of opinion and to work towards a common understanding. Your story of a situation may be different than mine, but then we have different experiences of life.

I can give my version of an event without making you look ridiculous, and vice versa.

• What gets said in the room stays in the room: keeping confidences is crucial. If people suspect their stories will be broadcast after the meeting, no one will share.

Certain rituals can enhance respectful listening. I often use Tibetan cymbals or *tingshas* to begin a storytelling session or meeting because of their calming effect. If debate has run overtime, the clear chime of the tingshas calls people back to attention. Some groups pass a baton or other object to single out the speaker and ensure no one else speaks at the same time. Many Native American traditions use a "talking stick" during council meetings. Holding it allows each council member to present his perspective or sacred point of view.

Places for sharing stories do not have to be elaborate. Your usual meeting spot is fine, but you should avoid spaces where outsiders can easily intrude or interrupt. Reception areas and lunchrooms may be good for gossip, but they are not conducive to productive storytelling.

If your organization or team is just beginning to try on storytelling for size, ensure constructive feedback for narrators. A closing ritual or pattern might include an affirmation for the speaker who has just taken a big risk in sharing a story. In a safe environment, stories can be deeply moving, providing insights about people, processes and situations that no one has previously recognized. It is what binds relationships and the reason why storytelling is so powerful. ❧

Strange Bedfellows

"I should tell you that I have an official Storyteller's License. A friend made it up and taped it to the wall over my desk. This license gives me permission to use my imagination in rearranging my experience to improve a story, so long as it serves some notion of Truth."

Robert Fulghum. [36]

M Y SON HAS A GENIUS for telling whoppers. He started young. At age three, on a family visit to the beach, James wandered off to find an audience. When we finally caught up with him half an hour later, he had a group enthralled with his tales. There was considerable consternation when James' Dad stepped forward to claim his wayward son; James had just finished telling his audience about the time his father lost his legs at sea to a shark.

Now a young man, James still can't resist an audience. His training as a Shakespearean actor has only served to enhance his narrative skills and propensities. Being his mother, I sometimes have a misplaced sense of responsibility for what I regard as outlandish behaviour. His stories sound suspiciously like lying to me. When confronted about his stories, James' usual response is to look wounded, especially if someone else is listening to our conversation. "I was only being metaphorical," he says. The truth and storytelling make for strange bedfellows.

REAL STORIES AREN'T ALWAYS "CORRECT"

You know what it's like to listen to a raconteur: he's like the fisherman who caught a fish THIS BIG. Did he actually catch a fish? Probably. Was it THIS BIG? Unlikely. But that doesn't diminish the delight both of you take in the story.

I am an advocate for real stories—the kind that emerge from your everyday experience. Your understanding of what happened may, however, be different than what *actually* happened. You know this from personal experience: your version of an event can differ markedly from another participant's, especially if that person is your partner or another family member. Whose version is the Real one? Who's telling the Truth? And what's wrong with a little embroidery?

Physician Rachel Naomi Remen has listened to thousands of stories in her counselling work with medical practitioners and cancer patients. Chronicled in her books *Kitchen Table Wisdom* and *My Grandfather's Blessings*, the stories demonstrate that what counts is being genuine. Using the metaphor of a video camera, Remen reminds readers that although an outside and impartial source might show a different story than the one you told, your story is a reflection of your experience. It is real for you at this moment. When you narrate a story, you are inviting your listeners into your life, allowing them, as Remen says, to see something familiar through new eyes.[37]

Deliberately misleading people with your stories is clearly self-defeating—think of all the lies you would have to tell to explain that story about missing work because you injured yourself, when in fact you were at the golf course! Business literature is filled with cautionary tales about people who told fabulous stories to make themselves look good, only to be caught out in fabrications.

Robert Fulford narrates some infamous examples of storytelling taken to extremes in his book, *The Triumph of Storytelling*. One of these is the story of Grey Owl, the Englishman Archie Balaney who passed himself off as a North American Indian in the first half of the 20th century. A more recent example is that of James Frey, author of the book, *A Million Little Pieces*. In the book Frey portrays himself as a man in recovery from addictions. Only after book sales soared did the world discover Frey's so-called life story was riddled with gross exaggeration and outright fabrications. He is unlikely to be taken seriously in the publishing world again.

TRUSTWORTHY TALES—A CONTRADICTION IN TERMS?

Let's say I am at a staff social and hear a story about a male manager who was witnessed criticizing a female employee. The person telling me this story, a woman, has come to the conclusion the manager is abusive toward women. In narrating this event for me, her personal outlook colours her interpretation of what she witnessed. Being a woman who may have felt victimized herself in the past, her "take" on the manager's interaction with the employee might be different from another witness, say a male employee raised in the school of hard knocks. And then, of course, there is the female employee who was seen being criticized: she might narrate this story from the perspective of a victim at the mercy of a heartless manager, or from any one of several other perspectives. Whose story will I believe?

Each of the parties in this little drama has a vested interest in narrating the story so that we, the audience, take his or her side. Can you ever really trust another person's story? Anthropologist Clifford Geertz, a master storyteller himself, has pointed out that invariably the narrator's attitudes and cultural context will influence the way he tells his story. Similarly, as a listener you have your own cultural biases through which you filter the story. Getting at "the truth" is an elusive goal.[38]

In spite of our tendency to want people to see things our way, this kind of self-centered narrative does not always occur—a testament to the integrity and self-awareness of some people. In the story just narrated, the employee who was seen being criticized might own up to having missed deadlines because she works two jobs to make ends meet, and the manager might confess that he is in the midst of a messy divorce, and his unresolved angst has got the best of him. As a witness, my informant (the storyteller) could attempt to see the event from the perspectives of the other participants, trying to remove her own bias in the process.

Your task as storyteller is to be as genuine as you can; mine as listener is to suspend judgment long enough to really "hear" the story. When you have finished, I can always ask clarifying questions. If your intent is to convey a value you hold near and dear—being true to the team for instance—the correctness of your story's details will be less important than if you have enhanced my sense of belonging or inspired me to support the team. A lecture would have gone in one ear and out the other. Your story, on the other hand, will stay with me for some time, a reminder that we are in this together. ❧

Sympathetic Connections

"Don't be slick. These are Americans. They've seen slick.
Be yourself—they haven't seen that."

Peggy Noonan.[39]

OVER COFFEE, WARREN REDMAN is entertaining me with the
story of one of his clients, a salesman. Warren is the author
of *The 9 Steps to Emotional Fitness* and has developed a counselling
methodology that can be taught to, and by, anyone with a passion
for self-growth. Part of his coaching with clients involves a narrative process. I listen avidly as he describes a client who was ready to
throw in the towel. The man had been unsuccessful in sales and was
barely earning enough to support his wife and two children.

After two years of working with Warren, the salesman was not only
earning a good living but was invited to give the professionals at head
office a talk on how to improve their sales. He didn't give them the
standard how-to talk about making lists or "strategizing for sales success". Instead, he encouraged them to know and listen to themselves,
so that they could tell their own story. He told them his, including
the frustrations and mistakes, and the audience was captivated.

Warren's story of a man narrating a compelling story for his peers
is a reminder that persuasive storytelling is not the same as teaching
or preaching. Notice that the man refrained from delivering a "how-
to" lecture for his colleagues. This begs the question: what makes
a story persuasive, especially if all stories have a little bit of Peter
Pan's Neverland about them? The answer to this question rests partly

with the story's construction (whether it has a logical flow) and the meaning listeners attribute to the story.

It was the ancient Greek writer and philosopher Aristotle who said a good story has a beginning, middle and end, and that you have to structure your stories to make them credible and easy to follow. If your listeners lose the thread of your story, they will lose interest period, and you will be less likely to persuade. Ensuring a logical structure means taking time to think through your objectives before narrating your story. The adoption of a wisdom story format with its sequence of "what it was like, what happened, and what it's like now" can facilitate delivery.

Aristotle had another sage piece of advice for the would-be storyteller: establish a sympathetic connection with your audience. Often applied to a story in which someone experiences a turn of fortune, Aristotle demonstrated how to help the audience become part of the storyline in a play. Typically, the main character or protagonist experiences some dire change in circumstances (reversal) and then through a journey of introspection and increasing self-awareness, comes to a place of recognition. Nearly everyone in an audience has been through a process like this. As the performers act out the play, audience members step into the narrative and "connect" with the characters.

The story narrated by Warren is an example of reversal and recognition: it is the story of a man who turned his life around, and who then shared his story with colleagues so that they could grow in wisdom as well. The salespeople listening to the narrative would be familiar with the fears, frustrations and struggles peculiar to a sales career, and would therefore connect with the narrator. In turn, his honesty helps them become more honest about their own imperfections. Many screenplays use this same technique to help the audience connect with the story's actors.

In a business setting, you could resort to something similar to explain a change in the company's direction. Perhaps external threats to the business have made the change necessary. As the narrator, you can create a sympathetic connection with other employees by telling a story that puts them into the story as participants. This entails explaining the turn of fortune the company is going through, being honest about its mistakes and what needs to change, and explaining what their role will be going forward.

Establishing clear structure and using the theatrical device of a turn of fortune are both techniques for involving and persuading the audience. Peggy Noonan's observation reminds us that being real, rather than slick, is what really counts. My experience of conducting workshops on storytelling confirms this. The best storytellers in the room are not the professional performers and speakers, although they may be practiced at speaking in front of audiences. Instead, the most convincing stories often come from those participants who have no stage training and who can only, therefore, be true to what they have known in life.

As a novice storyteller developing your skills in a workplace setting, sincerity will convince your audience better than stylish delivery. And if you find yourself sharing stories with larger groups, these ground rules will help:

- Take time to find out who will be in your audience and what matters to them; research how they speak to each other and use language at the right level for that audience. This means being careful to avoid the use of "management-speak" or technical language that would obscure your message.
- Talk about other people's accomplishments rather than dwelling exclusively on your own, and if you do talk about yourself, talk about who you are and what matters to you, not about what you do or your achievements.
- If you want to be persuasive, do not criticize others in your presentation, or you will call into doubt everything you have just said, and probably everything you say afterwards.
- For much the same reasons, do not overstate your case.[40]

Facts-based lectures or slick presentations have their place, but convincing storytelling is ultimately a reflection of your vision and sincerity. Like the salesman who was honest about his process of self-discovery, the best preparation is to learn to listen to yourself. ❧

Detail Counts

God is in the details.

Advice every student receives on entering a faculty of architecture. [41]

I F YOU HAVE EVER HAND STITCHED a garment or painstakingly whittled the feathers of a wooden bird, you already know that detail counts. An accumulation of hundreds of tiny, evenly-spaced stitches makes the garment stronger and more beautiful to behold. Dozens of fine strokes with a carving knife result in feathers that almost look real. The same can be said for stories: many small details make for stories that sound and feel real.

Find Your Voice at Work begins with the story of Adi watching as I unpack a bundle of shadow puppets in Indonesia. By using the present tense and describing my awkward gestures separating one puppet from another, I create a word picture for readers. You can almost see the long, thin limbs of the puppets with their horn handles. Almost put your fingers through the tooled surface of the Mountain puppet. As Adi names the puppets, each one assumes an individual persona.

Imagine how different the story would have sounded had I left out all the details that give it a uniquely Javanese flavour. In that case, this is the story you would have heard: "I was living and working in Indonesia. On one of my trips for work, I commissioned some shadow puppets. Shortly after they arrived, I unpacked them for my boss, Adi. When I handed him the largest of the puppets, he told me this story…"

Unpacking the puppets is still a story, but missing are the details that enliven the narrative and help listeners experience it with their senses. Without this level of information, you're left wondering, "What is she talking about? What does a shadow puppet look like?"

Details add texture. You find yourself squinting to imagine the Mountain puppet with its finely tooled surface. You can visualize and almost touch the attenuated limbs of the other puppets. My encounter with Adi is made more insightful by my acknowledgment that I am awkward with these puppets, and unable to name them. My lack of familiarity is proof positive I am the foreigner who has much to learn about Indonesian culture.

Most employees have experience with using narrative detail in constructing STAR responses for behavioural descriptive interviews. The interviewer has a checklist of qualities and skills she is looking for in a particular staff position, and asks questions to find out how you might handle situations that are likely to arise in her workplace. If it's a sales position you're after, she might inquire: Tell me about a time you had to deal with an angry customer.

In responding, you use the STAR outline: Situation, Task, Action and Result. For Situation, you explain when and where the incident took place, what happened and who was involved. Task refers to your role in managing the angry customer. What task or opportunity were you presented with? Action is what you did to try to resolve the situation, and Result refers to the outcome of your action and what you learned personally from handling the incident. By the time you've covered all your bases with a STAR answer, you've woven a story with a wealth of detail.

Adding texture or details to a story doesn't require an Honours degree in English literature. I have heard hundreds of artful stories narrated by people who lacked formal educations but had a gift for making their stories come alive. This next story is courtesy of a man who works at a local Costco. Costco is a member-owned grocery chain; it's not unusual for members to be interested in the chain's employees and operations. Gerry stocks shelves and moves product, and he's an enthusiastic employee who likes to promote the company and the benefits of membership. Gerry is also a "character" with a chequered career—a euphemism for the fact that for most of his adult life, he has struggled with substance abuse. Recently Gerry got help for his addictions. I'll let Gerry tell you his story.

"I was out in the far parking lot at work having a smoke break. Just enjoying my smoke and not thinking about much of anything. These two ladies approached in a car. I could tell they were deliberately coming my way by the way they headed for me. Then I saw they were two customers I've got to know over the past few months. I hadn't seen them in a while because they must be going to the new store that opened in the northwest of the city. They used to come and talk to me when I was restocking the shelves.

One of the ladies—did I tell you they were sisters?—one of the ladies rolls down her window and says how glad they are to see me. I always looked forward to our talks; they seemed really interested in me. I kinda missed not seeing them these last few months.

Well, there they are, all smiles, while I finish my smoke. One of them tells me I look better than they can ever remember. Healthier and happier, she says. Yeah, I say, and then—I don't know, it just seems right—I tell them that I'm two months clean and sober and that my life has changed. Then they start crying—big tears, man!—and the other sister says they've been praying for me all these months. They could see there was something wrong in my life, and they've been praying I would get help.

I didn't know there was anyone who cared enough about me to pray for me. It got me thinking. They're strangers really; just two customers at work. I can still see them crying and happy at the same time."

Details make what could have been a mundane work story, a narrative rich with meaning. We learn about the who, what, where, when and why of the encounter: at Costco, not the new store but the old one; in the far parking lot away from the crowds; Gerry, relaxing and having a smoke, just being; and two ladies in a car and members of Costco who have been monitoring his well-being for months, overjoyed that this man who was struggling has found some peace.

Gerry doesn't need to add, "I feel grateful" because as a listener, you have already gathered as much. As he narrates the story, you begin to share his amazement, and you can almost hear the awe in his voice.

When I first sat down to begin writing the stories in this book I confided to a friend that I didn't want my cynicism about corporate life to intrude on the book. I wanted the stories to sound fresh and full of hope. She listened to me and then offered this suggestion: "Why don't you write every story from a place of love?" The cynics out there may regard this as silly, but it worked for me. When I write from a place of affection for my subject and reader, the details of the story come easily. I am intent on making the act of listening to the story a joyful or thoughtful one for you. Details help in creating the right setting for the audience.

Even when I feel critical of my subject, I still try to imagine what it feels like for him. When I can convey what matters to him with small details of his gestures, actions or words, or where we were and why, suddenly the mundane becomes memorable. That "story" becomes *almost* real. ❧

Storytelling Dice

"Learn to write about the ordinary. Give homage to old coffee cups, sparrows, city buses, thin ham sandwiches. Make a list of everything ordinary you can think of. Keep adding to it. Promise yourself, before you leave the earth, to mention everything on your list as least once in a poem, short story, newspaper article."

Natalie Goldberg. [42]

A RTISTS AND WRITERS have a lot in common with storytellers, including the office variety of raconteur. Sometimes you feel like you've run out of ideas, or the ones you have don't work. If you are short on stories and you need one right now, it's time to throw the dice.

When my children were young and I desperately needed a break, I would book one week each summer at an art college to study drawing or ceramics. One year, I had a teacher who had us mark up sugar cubes as though they were dice. One die was for the drawing device we would use. If you threw a one, then your next drawing had to be in pencil; a two meant it was in charcoal, a three in pen and ink, and so on. The second die was to help decide whether you would draw for 30 seconds or 30 minutes; whether the model would be reclining or moving about. Throwing the dice took all the angst and guesswork out of drawing and made it possible to experiment and generate a lot of work quickly.

To create your own game of storytelling dice, draw up a list of

everyday items you could use as story reference points. A quick
list could include: coffee cups, mail, taxi drivers, couriers, Monday
morning meetings, and photocopy machines. There are legions of
stories about photocopy jams and the heroes who fix them. So too
about office coffee cups stacked under *"wash your own dishes"* signs.

Let's say I decide that a "three" on the die represents taxi drivers, and I throw a three. I could tell you the story of Achmad, an
illiterate taxi driver who gave me a hair-raising ride in Jakarta.
During our 30 minutes together he told me his story, a moving
testament to living in the moment and learning to trust in the
Unseen. At the time, my own trust levels were low and my ability
to "be present", minimal. Our drive was also memorable because
he was driving at breakneck speeds, five abreast in three lanes
of traffic, and probably thinking "Inshah Allah" to himself as he
careened between cars. I prayed fervently that this Unseen power
was going to keep us safe!

In *Writing Down the Bones*, author Natalie Goldberg suggests
periodically asking yourself a Big Question to clarify your reasons for writing. Rephrasing Goldberg's question for storytellers, it
would go like this:

Why should I tell stories? Or *Why be so foolish as to tell stories?*

1. Because your employees and colleagues don't want to be lectured
   to; tell a story instead.
2. Because you can be real with a story and people will respect you
   for it.
3. Because you think you have something worth saying (Now,
   what was it?).
4. Because you feel someone has to say "it", and a story is a better
   way to say it than a speech from the boss.
5. Because your family or teachers or an ex-partner belittled you
   for telling stories, and now you're getting even.
6. Because you were terrified of speaking as a kid and young adult,
   and now you are working through your fear in order to share

what matters to you, in the hopes that it will also be meaningful for other people.

7. Because you are secretly determined to create a more level playing field at work, and stories are a great way to do that.
8. Because people remember stories, not dry data and lists of facts. So tell a story instead.

You could now generate stories to go with each of the foregoing points. Let's pick point 6: telling a story about overcoming fear. Here is one of mine. At the outset of my architectural studies, I took a course in improvisational theatre so that my fear about speaking publicly wouldn't overwhelm me during studio presentations. This seemed illogical to my fellow students; they informed me a drafting or drawing class would have been more to the point.

In one improv class, the drama teacher created a zany office scenario with a boss, a desk, a telephone that kept ringing and a hapless employee asking for a raise. Every time the employee had mustered up enough courage to ask for the raise, the phone would ring, and the boss would interrupt. Working through scenarios like this one helped me over the worst of my fear when it came to speaking publicly. It also taught me that storytelling is supposed to be fun. You're allowed to be silly and even a little outrageous when you tell stories.

When generating new ideas and stories, remember not to edit too soon—consider possibilities, write them down if you like, test them with a friend or colleague, but don't worry if your story is a "good" one early on, or if anyone else will like it. Just put it out there and then reflect on the narrative before you get out your shears.

By working through exercises like these, you will come to appreciate that fodder for storytelling is all around you. Record it all, even the small stuff. Keep a desk diary, or one on your bedside table. Enter ideas in your personal organizer. Learn to observe and listen and Be Present! as that taxi driver in Indonesia reminded me 20 years ago.

Let storytelling teach you about life and life about storytelling. ✺

Inspiration for the Journey

What is truer than the truth? The story.

Jewish wisdom.

I MAGINE BEING PUT ON THE SPOT and asked for a story at the next team meeting. The prospect of coming up with your own story may be intimidating. Fortunately, there are hundreds of examples you can draw on from books and films. I honed my skills as a storyteller by telling folktales for children in schools. Only when I had become comfortable with other people's stories did I begin to write and tell my own.

For any given life situation, whether correcting a child or explaining new behaviour required during a transition at work, there is a story you could borrow from someone else. It might be a classical Greek writer like Homer or an author featured on the latest *Oprah* show. My advice is to read widely, borrow liberally unless the author expressly forbids it, and always remember to acknowledge your source in the telling.

World literature offers much for the aspiring storyteller. What follows is a short list of resources for inspiring stories.

FICTION

Classical literature abounds in stories with a moral point of view for use in the workplace or community setting. My favourite classical sources include *The Odyssey* and *The Iliad* by Homer and stories and myths from a variety of ancient cultures. Children's versions of these myths are often more accessible to your audience than original translations. These stories remind us that heroes are frequently unlikely candidates for the part, and not every story has a fairytale ending. Think of the story of the Trojan War from *The Iliad*, and the wanderings of the ancient Israelites in the desert of Sinai (fiction to some, history for believers). Narratives about being lost at sea or wandering in the wilderness make for great stories about finding self and building community.

Proverbs are quick and handy sources for the would-be storyteller. You can spin a story from an ancient proverb or modern koan to throw light on a current situation. Let's say you are addressing a source of workplace conflict and you want your colleagues to overcome their differences. Here's a Chinese proverb that could support your approach:

Convert great quarrels into small ones,
and small ones into nothing.[43]

Folklore, whether written by the Brothers Grimm or more contemporary folklorists like Jane Yolen is rich in imagery and moral content. Contemporary fiction and film include characters who exemplify both moral fibre and quirkiness. Think of Spock from *Star Trek*, the unflappable semi-alien who is troubled by a human's conscience and intuition, or R2-D2, the droid who provides comic relief and heroic gestures in *Star Wars*. Comic books and cartoons have added to the collection with figures like Charlie Brown and Lois Lane. Pick figures and situations that are meaningful for you and that support your intentions for the story.

NON-FICTION

War stories and adventure tales provide storytellers with content for examining the human condition and demonstrating what makes or breaks a team. Being a keen hiker and having trekked in Nepal, my favourite stories include tales of mountain adventures, like *Seven Years in Tibet* by Heinrich Harrer, *Into Thin Air* by Jon Krakauer and *The Snow Leopard* by Peter Matthiessen. Biography and autobiography are equally fruitful terrain for the narrator in search of tales with a moral point of view.

In the last few years there has been an awakening in business circles about the power of story. One of the best examples, choc-a-block with stories that the authors encourage readers to use, is *The Heart of Change* (John P. Kotter and Daniel S. Cohen); Cohen has subsequently published *The Heart of Change Field Guide*. Other, recent examples include Robert Fulford's collection, *The Triumph of Narrative*, and Malcolm Gladwell's books, *The Tipping Point* and *Blink*.

Inspirational and self-help literature is an especially rich vein for stories. My favourite sources are Rachel Naomi Remen's books *Kitchen Table Wisdom* and *My Grandfather's Blessings*, Warren Redman's *Recipes for Inner Peace* and *The 9 Steps to Emotional Fitness*, and Ernest Kurtz and Katherine Ketcham's book on storytelling and the search for meaning, *The Spirituality of Imperfection*.

Story, and its applications in community development, has become a specialized area called Appreciative Inquiry (AI), a strengths-based approach to organizational development. Organizations that use AI find it a powerful process for affirming direction and improving relationship building. Typically, a meeting will start with a story from one person at the table. That person might describe a recent challenge and how she overcame it. By consistently observing this kind of sharing at each meeting, everyone in the group becomes more familiar with each other's strengths and values. The non-profit world recognized the power of story long before the business sector; a quick search on the web will reward the interested story-teller with a multitude of resources.

There are a few caveats to consider in your search for stories. I love the stories found in Eastern and Western religious sources, but if you are going to narrate one of these, remember to account for your audience. Storytelling is not meant to be moralizing, although you may want to convey a moral point of view. Ditto for political stories, which your audience may construe as being partisan. If you select a story that resonates with some deep emotional experience, and you cannot narrate it without becoming upset, it might be wise to reserve the story until you have enough emotional distance from the past. For more information on the do's and don'ts of using stories, visit Doug Stevenson's website, Story Theatre International, *www.dougstevenson.com*.

If there is one metaphor that sticks with me, and which I often use to give my listeners inspiration for the journey, it is this Indonesian proverb:

Sedikit, sedikit menjadi bukit.
Little by little you build a mountain.

Learning to tell stories is like building a mountain—it takes time! ✀

Stage Fright

You dare your Yes—and experience a meaning
You repeat your Yes—
and all things acquire a meaning.
When everything has a meaning
how can you live anything but a Yes?

Dag Hammarskjöld.

WHAT IF YOU DID JUST ONE THING today to overcome your fear of storytelling? That one act might be sitting down with someone who is having a bad day at work and sharing your experience in a similar situation. Driving the kids to baseball practice you could invent a story about a little girl or boy who overcomes the doubters to hit a home run. You could decide to promote storytelling at the dinner table by encouraging family members to tell a story about their day. Each of these activities would develop your storytelling confidence.

Feeling uncomfortable about narrating stories in front of others is perfectly normal. It has been said that most people's greatest fear is public speaking. Reframe your storytelling by thinking of it as a chance to share ideas with friends in community.

When I was a student of life-drawing, we were obliged to draw on large sheets of paper—18 by 24 inches, or even 24 by 36 inches. We were told to fill the page with the image. It was a way of forcing us to overcome our hesitation about putting charcoal to paper. The bigger the sheet, the more the energy required to fill it—big, sweeping curves to draw the model posing in front of us.

Tell stories like you would fill a large sheet of paper, as though there were no boundaries. Use words you haven't used before, tell stories you never thought to tell. Be mischievous! If you start from a place of assuming no one wants to hear your stories, you will defeat yourself. Do you have a conviction about a story? Honour that conviction and share it.

There are many ways to diminish your stage fright and enjoy the storytelling process. A few include:

- Join a speaking group like Toastmasters, or take a speaking or storytelling course at a local college.
- Organize storytelling evenings in your home. Invite like-minded friends or colleagues.
- Tell all kinds of stories—folktales and examples of stories written by other people, nonsense tales and victim narratives, stories of hope and stories of discouragement (your own, and from books and films).
- Make a list of possible topics, write these on scraps of paper, and have people draw topics from a hat. These could be fun topics (everyone could be asked to tell a story about a computer that crashed) or more practical topics related to your work or community affiliation.
- Bring together a storytelling circle—put a candle in the middle—trust that everyone will share something wonderful, without any prompting or organizing on your part; say, "Tell us a story about... overcoming fear, a kind deed at work, volunteering at the local homeless shelter with your colleagues, that time you made a mistake..."

Think of every story you tell as a gift or a good deed that might enrich someone else's life. Don't ask, "Will they like me?" Wonder instead, "Can I make a difference in someone's life with this story?" Every time you narrate a story, it is a chance to share some experience, strength and hope with other people. In the process, you will be affirming your own worth. Most of us are pretty hard on ourselves; we forget our achievements and qualities when rehearsing our mistakes. By sharing a tale or two, you are being good to yourself and good to others in one fell swoop. ❧

Summary V

1. Organic stories sound heartfelt rather than concocted. The simplest way to narrate one is to use a wisdom story format: to tell a story about "what it was like, what happened, and what it's like now."

2. Before you introduce storytelling for your team or department, ensure you have created a welcoming environment. Rituals can facilitate this process.

3. There's a difference between telling the truth and narrating a story. The Storyteller's License permits you to embroider your tale with details, as long as you remain faithful to your understanding of the event.

4. A persuasive story has a clear beginning, middle, and end, making it easy for listeners to follow and connect the dots.

5. Your listeners may not remember dry facts but they will recall details. When crafting a wisdom story, include details about people, the situation and location. An easy way to ensure you have this kind of detail is to use the same questions any journalist or writer would: who, what, where, when, why.

6. Learn to give homage to the ordinary. Ideas for stories are all around you. To be compelling, your stories do not need to be sensational or heroic.

7. Overcome your stage freight by joining a storytelling or speaking group. Practicing in a safe setting will assuage your jitters.

Section VI

Storytelling Organizations

"You don't have to change much—just everything!"

12 step wisdom regarding the amount of personal
effort necessary to turn a life around.

WHAT DOES IT TAKE to become a storytelling organization?
The short answer is a major cultural shift. Transforming
the organization with stories means transforming everything. This
is because storytelling organizations have three distinct qualities:
1. They are by nature inherently democratic, valuing stories from
   everyone.
2. Employees and managers adopt a big picture perspective, not a
   bits and pieces approach to their work.
3. People feel they are part of some greater whole, a community that appreciates their efforts and supports them in their
   learning.

WHAT'S YOUR ORGANIZATION LIKE?

Much has been written about creating more innovative and
change-ready organizations, and the principles that apply in those
situations also apply to storytelling organizations. Enterprises
become more innovative when everyone contributes on a regular
basis to the bin of innovative ideas. Change is embraced when the
staff feels part of the process, rather than being acted upon. In both
cases, leadership provides the impetus behind the cultural shift to
a storytelling organization, recognizing that it can't possibly do it
all alone.

Initial attempts to introduce storytelling could originate with the Human Resources Department or individual managers. HR can lead the way with a variety of initiatives that enrich individual and group learning. Self-directed learning groups would be an ideal entry point. This section describes several forms of peer, or self-directed learning, to illustrate the flexibility and power of this learning model. Small groups of motivated participants, meeting on a periodic or regular basis, result in new learning of benefit to the wider organization. Sharing stories during meetings strengthens a sense of belonging to a supportive community.

Other ways to introduce more storytelling into the organization include formal mentoring arrangements between more experienced employees and those coming up through the ranks. Some mentoring experts argue that mentoring is most effective when employees select their own mentors, either inside or outside the organization. Regardless of the methodology for introducing mentoring, once established, relationships between mentors and their protégés continue to bear fruit at an individual and organizational level, long after the formal mentoring contract expires.

Coaching that applies a narrative cycle is another effective method for engaging employees in storytelling. Warren Redman's model based on his award-winning book, *The 9 Steps to Emotional Fitness*, is described in this section. Warren uses storytelling to encourage people to own the need for change, especially for altering attitudes or workplace behaviours that limit progression. Standard management practices like performance reviews can be transformed with these same narrative techniques.

The kind of storytelling recommended here, with its focus on rigorous honesty in order to understand self and one's place in the world, requires qualities that some organizations seem to be short on: time for reflection, genuine respect for a diversity of opinions and contributions, and ethical behaviour. Paying lip service to these values while telling stories may lead management to believe it has conned the "masses", but you will never convince staff of management's sincerity when it comes to telling stories—employees know the real McCoy when they hear one.

Whether sanctioned by leadership or not, the initiative for sharing stories ultimately rests with individual employees who care about the creation of more hospitable and productive workplaces. Leadership's support makes it easier. Finding your voice at work is first and foremost an "inside job". Personal change of any magnitude requires self-reflection, honesty, concerted effort, mutual support and heartfelt intentions. Organizational change is equally demanding. As the stories in this collection demonstrate, the results are worth the effort. The question is: Are you and your organization ready? ❦

Deep Listening

"Why do I put such an emphasis on listening in the first place? Because I believe that listening opens the door to self-understanding, inner security, empowerment and ultimately the development of each individual to be the authentic, unique and greatest person he or she can be. In seemingly tiny ways, every time we listen something great happens. Relationships are transformed."

Warren Redman. [44]

THE DIN IN THIS SEMINAR ROOM has escalated with new arrivals, and there are now more people than chairs. This is a group of aspiring speakers with the extraverts far outnumbering the introverts. We have assembled to learn more about applying a narrative process to coaching. I sandwich myself into one of the last available seats at the back of the room and find myself next to a woman who is frowning. Over the noise, the Master of Ceremonies is trying to get our attention. Eventually she succeeds and now all eyes are on the speaker, Warren Redman. A tall, lean Englishman with a kind face and serene manner, he looks out of place in this room full of boisterous participants.

After sharing a humorous story about a painful experience with public speaking, Warren outlines his main topic for our workshop. He has developed a narrative process for coaching situations, and following a short but instructive introduction, he puts us to work. I am paired with the woman next to me. She is still frowning. We are to each take 10 minutes to share a story following Warren's five step narrative cycle. The noise in the room soundly rockets, and I invite my partner into a quiet corner of the hallway where we can be more at ease and hear each other without shouting. There are two armchairs and I sink into mine; my partner is perched on hers.

Her face is contorted by distress, as though the prospect of telling a story is intimidating her. I have been through this process before with Warren and find it to be full of wonder. The results are unpredictable but invariably enlightening. Our first step for working together today is for one of us to assume the coach's role; I volunteer to take this on. I sense this woman has something she needs to relate, even if she hasn't recognized it yet herself.

As per our instructions, she begins by creating an index of experiences. There are five subtitles or categories under which she can identify stories. The categories are work, leisure, education, relationships and life events. "How will I ever identify one or two experiences under each subtitle?" she laments. I suggest she start with the area that seems most immediate for her. In the next two minutes, she has written down brief notes for at least one experience in each category. Choosing an experience from her academic studies, she launches into her story.

In the ensuing 20 minutes, I hear a story full of pain and anguish, the description of an experience she has been carrying like a stone for years. It is a tale of betrayal and unfairness, of missed opportunities and failure. The story concerns one of her professors at university who marked her harshly on a major essay. In spite of her intentions to redress this, her courage failed and when she had the chance to speak up, she couldn't defend herself adequately. Long after she has graduated, this story still leaves her struggling with tears and feeling the universe is not fair.

My task is to listen without interrupting while she narrates her story. When she has finished relating the experience, I finally speak.

I clarify what I have heard, repeating elements of her story and asking if I have understood. Yes, she answers, it was just as I say.

We move on to the second stage of the narrative cycle. I invite her to write down her story in full and to read it back to me. My prompt for her is: What have you learned from this experience? She hesitates only momentarily and then pours out her feelings. When she should have stood up for herself, she was afraid. Having shared this, she writes down what she has learned.

Step three of the narrative cycle requires that she demonstrate her achievement. How might she use what she has learned about herself? As I listen carefully, inclining towards her so that I can hear her over the other groups in the hallway, she regrets she has previously failed to see that it was never about the professor at all; it was about her fear.

In the fourth stage I inquire what else she can learn from this experience. Suddenly the answer is crystal clear: to have carried around this resentment so long has been punishing, robbing her of joy and failing to change the underlying problem. If she wants to find peace, she will have to let go of her resentment.

In the final step, I ask what learning opportunities she plans to take up. Her anger and sorrow evaporate as she thinks about what she can do. She could write out her resentments each evening, putting them to bed rather than carrying them around for weeks and months at a time. She could take a course in self esteem, she could seek counselling to deal with her fear. There are a myriad of options.

The bell goes off, indicating it is time to return to the seminar room. I have not had time to share, but this seems inconsequential compared to the momentous experience of my partner. The energy in the room is calmer now. Warren inquires what participants have learned. Those at the front of the room monopolize the exchange at first and then from the back of the room, my partner finds the courage to put up her hand. She declares for the whole room to hear: "I feel like I have really been listened to for the first time in my life." There are tears in her eyes as she says this.

A coach can offer the gift of listening; it is as much a part of storytelling as the narrative itself. Too often, the coach is preoccupied with providing solutions, with "fixing" the client, rather than allowing her to find her voice. Warren Redman has made deep listening an essential element of his Emotional Fitness training courses for coaches and therapists. Forget about offering solutions or demonstrating how smart you are. Just be. Breathe deeply, relax, and incline your head to hear the other person's story. If you ask questions, do it to clarify, not to challenge or contradict.

When your colleague has finished her story, summarize what you have heard. Each encounter or coaching appointment is an opportunity to help another person gain insight into who she is and why she reacted to a situation in a particular way. By the simple act of listening to a story, you will be helping someone see herself in a new and more positive light. ❧

Elijah's Tale

"Give a man a fish, and you feed him for a day. Teach a man to fish, and you feed him for a lifetime."

Anonymous.

CY CHARNEY IS TALKING ABOUT his favourite topic, self-directed learning, and his enthusiasm is bubbling over as he shares the story of Elijah Racheku. Elijah is a black South African who grew up under the worst of apartheid and who has been an employee of South African Railways for several years. Cy is a successful management consultant in Canada, a white South African who emigrated more than 30 years. At first glance, the pair seem unlikely colleagues.

The two met as a result of Elijah's involvement with one of Cy's learning programs called Peer Mentoring® in North America, and the Peer Learning System in South Africa. The process was originally designed by Cy for middle managers in a first world culture. A South African company familiar with his model of self-directed learning picked it up and is delivering the program in that country. Its first client was South African Railways, and its first peer mentoring group was a group of black employees. Most were illiterate and spoke little or no English. Cy designed the process for middle managers, and he was initially sceptical it would succeed at the railway.

Being proven wrong has been a source of satisfaction for Cy. It turned out his peer mentoring process was ideally suited to this group of unionized workers from the railway, although no one suspected this at the beginning. Cy believes two factors made the program a success:

- Many people in the Black community of South Africa are self-directed learners, a result of years of apartheid during which they were cheated of an adequate education.
- Black people in South Africa come from an oral culture. Cy's process incorporates the sharing of experiences using different management tools. The storytelling aspect of peer mentoring has been a perfect fit with the railway workers' culture.

The impetus for introducing the program came as the result of a major rail strike which brought transportation and industry to a halt in South Africa. The railway's management was planning to privatize and outsource many functions, and the workers responded by locking up essential equipment. They were out long enough to force President Nelson Mandela to intervene personally. As part of the settlement to end the strike, management agreed to provide training for the workers and to desist from outsourcing their positions.

In the wake of the strike, management suggested several training alternatives to the black union's leadership. Most of these smacked of latent apartheid to the union: white teachers would deliver training to black workers. As Cy narrates this story, it becomes clear that these workers were ripe for exposure to new learning, and adamant that they would teach themselves. Only one training program permitted them to do so, and that was Cy's. Clive Price of Peer Learning in South Africa was the consultant who presented the proposal to the union.

Convincing the union to adopt a peer learning approach was not instantaneous. During negotiations Clive had to overcome the suspicion that his program was just a ploy by management to keep black workers in their place. But the decision was clinched when it was agreed that Clive would train a union employee to deliver the program to his peers. The membership of the union selected Elijah, an outspoken union activist with a high profile.

Elijah's story is a testament to the value of peer mentoring. With few formal communication skills when he first commenced training with Clive, today he is an articulate spokesman for his company and their training programs. Using the tools that go with the mentoring system, including Cy's book, *The Instant Manager*, Elijah introduced self-directed learning at the railway. His audience was composed of black workers who had missed out on an education in the old South Africa. He was so successful that the company sent him to Germany to learn ISO 9000; on his return, he helped implement it at the railway. Today he works in corporate human resources for the organization.

Cy will tell you that if he teaches a conventional "talk and chalk" type training session, not much is retained at the end of the day. On the other hand, if employees teach each other management principles and techniques, using Cy's tools as a reference, they remember as much as 95% of the teaching. With peer mentoring, colleagues come from across a company to form a group and train each other. The process is predicated on adult education principles that assume people are responsible for their own learning. Members of a peer mentoring group determine their training needs.

Elijah's job was one of facilitation as opposed to teaching. Working collaboratively with the unionized employees, he has provided volunteer learners with a proven process to ensure that time spent in training sessions is relevant and effective. Group members not only take ownership for their own learning, but they design action plans and ensure new skills are applied in the workplace. Meetings include sharing stories about how new skills are being used, what works and what doesn't.

In a busy workplace, employees and supervisors rarely find time to hold exchanges and think forward. Peer mentoring meetings are held monthly to ensure staff is responding proactively to challenges. The topic at a meeting might be improving an operational process, dealing with an angry customer or managing a disengaged employee. Each meeting is a jumping off point for swapping tips about how to handle the situation.

Cy and Elijah met about two years after peer mentoring was launched at the railway. In honour of a visit he made to South Africa, the union organized a special reception for Cy. With tears in his eyes, Cy listened to stories from the railway men about how their lives had been transformed by peer mentoring. The two men have kept in touch ever since.

Can a system of learning that works with illiterate black workers in post-apartheid South Africa be equally successful with employees in North America? Cy thinks so, and has successfully implemented Peer Mentoring® at a variety of corporate and non-profit organizations. All an organization needs are employees with a desire to learn and the ability to be self-directed. ❧

Letters from Rita

"While I've never been much of a gambler, I am willing
to wager that the concept of mentoring has been around
since the dawn of time. In the days of the Caveman,
the elders in the group must have mentored their youth
in survival skills or none of us would be around to talk
about it."

Shona Welsh. [45]

THOSE CAVEMEN SHONA WELSH is referring to undoubtedly
imparted their wisdom through stories. Some youth probably
made for more willing learners than others, and some mentors were
more successful in teaching hunting and life skills. Thank goodness
for wise mentors and willing learners!

The technical term for someone being mentored is "mentee".
I suspect some of us make for better mentees than others. I have a
mentor who must be a saint to work with me.

My mentor's name is Rita, and she's a dynamo. Rita holds down
a demanding job as the manager of alumni relations for the local
university's business school. She supports and leads a variety of
charitable efforts and is well known locally. Before cancer changed
her life a decade ago, she owned and managed an international ani-
mation supply company. In the 15 months that I have known her,
she has had cancer surgery twice. Somehow she still finds time to
mentor, consult with, encourage and support several people. Rita is
a mentor with a gift for storytelling.

Given Rita's busy schedule, one of the ways we connect is through email. Our correspondence tells a story about the unfolding of a mentoring relationship and the benefits of the process. I had known Rita for about two years before formally asking her to be my mentor. In preparation for approaching her, I prepared an elaborate proposal. You'd have thought I was after some work; its formality definitely caught her by surprise. Her response was polite but guarded: she would consider my request but needed time to review it in light of other commitments.

Email is a tricky way to build a relationship, but Rita has mastered the art. When she replied to confirm taking on the role of my mentor, her email began with a story from her personal life. One of her daughters had just married, and it was a joyous event. Narratives pulled from her family and professional life bring me into the warmth of her world. They also clarify her values about working with people.

In accepting the role of mentor, Rita outlined her understanding of a mentoring relationship and identified a potential obstacle. I had unrealistically high expectations that concerned her. Her reservations were conveyed with humour and a story or two about her experiences with other people who aimed so high they were hard to live with. We met for lunch and I offered to retreat from my tightly organized proposal, after which we both had a good laugh at my expense.

Like a lot of mentees, I say I want direction but I am not always amenable when it comes my way. It is those highfalutin expectations of mine getting in my way. As Rita likes to remind me, sometimes you just have to accept life on life's terms and "go with the flow".

Establishing a business hasn't come easily to me. I am familiar with the struggle, disappointments and elation of the entrepreneur. By way of encouragement, Rita sends me inspirational material, the kind of sentiments that women share. I am not sure what male mentors send their mentees but women can be remarkably upbeat and funny, and Rita has a funny bone. From jokes and comic strip-type cartoons, to heartfelt stories from her work with the community-based cancer support centre she co-founded, Wellspring Calgary, Rita stays in touch with those she mentors and befriends.

Rita has become the equivalent of my hunting and life skills mentor. Like most mentees, I won't need her mentoring forever. Pretty soon, it will be my turn to mentor others. This book is one of the fruits of her advice. As I move into the next phase of my professional development, I will be taking with me her funny and wise comments about business and life.

While Rita is a natural mentor, and I regard her as a rare find, there are like-minded people in every organization. Some mentors and mentees benefit from an orientation about what to expect. I certainly needed Rita's guidance. In her guide to establishing mentoring programs in organizations, *Mentoring the Future*, consultant Shona Welsh emphasizes the benefits of training for both parties. Even the best natural mentors appreciate opportunities to debrief with the program coordinator, and this debriefing usually takes the form of sharing stories. Eleventh-hour training needs often emerge during conversations between mentors and mentees, leading to follow up training for the mentee in a range of competencies.

Organizations that implement mentoring programs are the ultimate beneficiaries. Job applicants prefer to work where formal mentoring systems are in place, and an organization's commitment to mentoring often leads to improved retention. Mentoring also supports faster integration of new employees and reduces training costs. It enhances teamwork, innovation and continuous learning.

Perhaps the most significant advantage of mentoring for all parties is the transfer of knowledge around life skills, such as building healthy workplace relationships. It is hard to teach the "how-to" of relationship building in a traditional workshop setting. Stories are the ideal vehicle for conveying this kind of learning.

From the perspective of building a stronger community, mentoring is a forum for people to share their experience and hope—and it is one more way for you to use storytelling in your organization. ॐ

A Picture Paints
a Thousand Words

"The world is complex, dynamic, multidimensional; the
paper is static, flat. How are we to represent the rich visual
world of experience and measurement on mere flatland?"

Edward R. Tufte. [46]

THE SETTING IS A FACILITY in the Kananaskis range of the
Rocky Mountains. With the valley's peaks reminding us just
how small and insignificant we are in the grand order of things,
about 30 people have gathered for a one-day workshop with the
Co-design Group. It is a sunny day in early December, cold but not
yet the dead of mountain's winter, the kind of weather that makes
being outdoors still attractive. Leader Stan King is like a shepherd,
pulling his flock together to get the day's proceedings underway.
Dressed in warm corduroy pants and a knitted vest, he looks like
a gentleman hiker. In softly modulated tones that have retained a
hint of an English accent, he introduces our purpose, the redesign
of William Watson Lodge and its environs for handicapped users.
Dividing us into four groups, we scatter to different parts of the hall.
Drew, Bill and Merinda are leading the other groups.

Most people are familiar with some kind of participatory process,
if not in the workplace then through volunteer work. Co-Design
members are experts at promoting people's participation in the
design of their communities and workplaces. Almost thirty years

after I joined them as a volunteer artist, Co–Design is more active than ever at demonstrating that ordinary folk are quite capable of understanding planning concepts, articulating their needs, and helping to design the environments in which they reside and work.

I am a participant in Stan's group. During the morning session, Stan invites us to imagine what the existing lodge facility must be like for handicapped users. Although originally designed for people in wheelchairs, the lodge's facilities are not up–to–date by today's standards. Stan begins by asking us to observe the obstacles presented by the current building's design: "If you were in a wheelchair or using a walker, if you were blind or deaf, in what ways would you be inconvenienced by this building? Could you enjoy it the way the designers originally intended?"

We respond with stories, picking up on Stan's sensory cues. Imagine, he says, what sight or touch clues special needs users would require in this space. What auditory clues would make it easier for them to be in this environment? Is there anything distinctive about the taste and smells of this interior? And what about the mood you sense here, or in the adjacent buildings with overnight accommodation? How do people move about indoors and outside, on the wide pathways? How easy is it to be a handicapped user being moved from a vehicle into the lodge?

Our group's composition is diverse. There is the custodian who shovels the walks in winter, and the senior executive who is responsible for managing the entire provincial park. There are volunteers who support the special needs users, and interpretive guides who work throughout the park. One of our group is legally blind and another is in a wheelchair.

During our exchange of ideas, Stan is busy drawing the kinds of spaces we propose. Trained as an architect and a talented artist, he works in felt pen and quickly renders our ideas into recognizable forms on the paper in front of him. Someone is trying to imagine what it must be like for a blind person to walk the outdoor paths, using a cane to navigate. There are many changes in grade yet no directional clues for the unwary blind walker. Stan quickly draws an example of a pathway incorporating changes in paving texture, by way of grade-level indicators. Another member of our group recommends a "textured" map to aid in orientation to the site. Yet a third notes the pathways have steep drop offs, making them dangerous for wheelchair users and the blind; these sharp drops offs need to be modified to avoid injuries.

The site custodian relates a tale of budget cuts and their impact. There is no money for regular and timely clearing of snow on the pathways during winter, making them impassable for many special users. This observation stumps the group momentarily. We finally agree that representation needs to be made to the appropriate authorities, explaining the need for funding for this service, otherwise the handicapped will not come in winter. Stan annotates the drawing with this information.

By the middle of the afternoon there are dozens and dozens of drawings, each one associated with a story or image for the site's future use. The senior bureaucrat in the group is impressed with the quality of the discussion. After 20 years of constant use, the provincial government has recognized that it is time for facility improvements, and our workshop has generated the data required to prepare a business case for officialdom's consideration. Just as importantly, by bringing together staff and volunteers representing every aspect of the park, people have bonded. The Co-Design process has enabled us to identify our shared values on behalf of the special users of William Watson Lodge. Differences have dissolved in the participatory process, which brings out the best in us all.

The design establishment trains architects and planners to be the experts when it comes to designing buildings and spaces for public use. Other than supplying information and paying taxes to support construction, there is no place for the average citizen in conventional design projects. I know this from having studied to be an architect myself. Some of my readers could be levelling a similar criticism at their organizations' leadership: there is no place for the average employee in building a vibrant workplace community, even when leadership values its creation. All too often, upper management assumes this work is its preserve.

Participatory processes like Co-Design workshops cut through differences in status and rank to draw on people's strengths. Sharing our stories, a new vision for the site's redevelopment has taken shape—we can literally see it in the drawings. Each drawing has been annotated by the artist with our suggestions for change. By the time we have finished, there is a sense of ownership among the group for making the change happen. This result is very different from the one that takes place when leadership mandates change without meaningful input from the people who will live with the consequences.

The way to create a community, be it a lodge for handicapped visitors or a workplace of thousands, is to adopt a big picture perspective of the whole you want to create with your change initiatives. All those drawings Co-design created constitute that big picture in a literal and metaphorical sense: literally, with the drawings and metaphorically, with collaborative effort and storytelling. The "whole" is more than a physical structure or a place for generating profit for the organization's owners and shareholders. It is a place where people learn, grow, and socialize. It has emotional and spiritual dimensions as well as logistical and physical ones.

It is not possible to create a community without the active contribution of the people who live and work there. Ask them for their stories of what constitutes hospitable, harmonious environments, and listen carefully to their reflections.[47] Their answers will provide you with the clues you need to make your organization a coherent whole—the kind of environment where people love to work and innovation is commonplace. ✺

Big Questions

"Peer learning circles (PLC's) create experiential learning with a process of reflection, discussion and discovery. This increases individual capacity and enhances group collaboration. Your learning will be immeasurably increased if you keep an open mind and acknowledge your own limited knowledge…"

Keith Seel and Andrée Iffrig. [48]

YOU COULD NEVER ACCUSE Keith Seel of drifting through life. He asks provocative questions, the kind that make most of his listeners uncomfortable. Keith has a purpose. He is passionate about lifelong learning and leadership development, and has dedicated his career to increasing these capacities in non-profit organizations. The Director for the Institute for Nonprofit Studies at Mount Royal College, this morning he has doffed his suit jacket for an animated exchange in his office about why the world needs Peer Learning Circles or PLC's. Ignoring the cup of hot tea at his side, Keith is responding to my questions about the utility of PLC's.

"So what if non-profit governance boards don't change the way they function? They've muddled along this far. Who wants to spend extra time "reflecting" on what it means to be a board governor? Most volunteer board members find it hard just to set aside two or three hours a month for a regular board meeting, never mind attending extra meetings for developmental purposes. And now you want them to become reflective about their role! What's the return for investing in a board's capacity?"

Keith is ready for me, responding with stories to my questions. "If you're wondering if it's worthwhile to invest in enhancing the capacity of governance volunteers," he counters, "just consider the story of the Developmental Disabilities Resource Centre (DDRC). It's becoming a national leader in delivering services for people with special needs, people born with Down Syndrome or who are autistic. A little over a decade ago, it was moribund—it had lost sight of the agency's original mandate, its funding had been drastically reduced by government, and it faced an uncertain future. The urgency of the situation forced the board to review the agency's mission and values. A decision was made to promote inclusion and independence for people with developmental disabilities. Today, the board is at the forefront of changes, thanks to a commitment to engaging in discussion and reflection on what it means to govern the agency."

In the ensuing hour's conversation, Keith takes me through the how-to of PLC's and explains their benefits to organizations. A peer learning circle is a type of peer mentoring group that comes out of a model for participatory development conceived in Sweden more than a century ago. I am familiar with peer mentoring, but not this variation. Keith has been testing the concept, first with groups of executive directors and more recently with governance boards.[49] More permutations are planned for the future as he explores the use of PLC's in other organizational settings.

To experience a PLC, imagine that you are part of a group of 9 to 12 people. All of you are leaders in your respective fields. Each session of the PLC is facilitated by two trained facilitators. Your group's purpose is to deepen your understanding of what leadership means in your context. If you are serving with a board of governors, what does it mean to govern an agency or company? If you are part of a senior management team, what does it mean to lead in the big sense of the word? Keith cautions that leadership is not just about numbers. If you spend all your time worrying about financial matters or outputs, your focus is too narrow. Leadership has different dimensions, and leading means exercising them all.

Let's say your group is meeting to explore the strategic dimension of governance.[50] This is an aspect that frequently gets short shrift in organizations. To kick things off, the facilitators provide direction regarding the agenda, and they ensure an atmosphere of respectful sharing and listening. The group then breaks up into smaller groups to reflect on the following kinds of questions:

- What capacity or competencies does a governance board need in order to envision a direction for the organization?
- What role does an individual governor have in shaping or sharpening priorities?
- In what ways would a board reinforce a strategic focus, as opposed to a financial one?

In your small group what you'll hear by way of responses to these big questions are stories of your peers' experiences in serving on boards and in other kinds of organizations. Stories about what worked and what didn't. Stories about bitter disappointments and amazing results. After spending some time reflecting in your small group, everyone reconvenes to share reflections. In the discussion, new learning takes place not just at an individual level, but for the entire group. More stories are shared. Effective boards know how to collaborate between board members as well as with the agency, and the PLC process of reflection, discussion and discovery enhances this kind of collaboration. It leads to innovative thinking and strategic decision making.

Keith is convinced that governance can and should be more than an exercise in accountability and transparency. PLC's are the vehicle for getting there. An academic who values rigour in his research, Keith has devised a pre- and post-evaluation for ascertaining the effectiveness of the learning circle. Participants have been positive about their experience with the process.

Our meeting drawing to an end, Keith makes his final point:
People who join non-profit boards want to make a difference;
they're not satisfied with the status quo. Participatory approaches
offer a means for challenging conventional ideas and creating conditions for change.

If it works for leaders in the non-profit sector, it can work
for corporate "leaders" as well. You will need an open mind and
a willingness to entertain big questions, the kind for which there
are no easy answers. You will have to acknowledge your own, limited knowledge as you become engaged in the peer learning circle
process. The stories you share and hear will change how you see
yourself, your organization and the world. ❧

Development from
the Ground Up

"The central concept of people-centered development is
quite simple. It is an approach to development that looks
to the creative initiative of people as the primary development resource and to their material and spiritual well-being
as the end that the development process serves."

David C. Korten and George Carner. [51]

P EOPLE MILL ABOUT in a large room, the proceedings predictably late in starting. There has been a last-minute glitch with
the printing, and most guests at this two-day conference still don't
have copies of the teaching case study we are about to discuss. I
fuss about the missing publication and the lateness of our start—a
Westerner expecting her Asian counterparts to share her obsession
with timeliness. My boss rebukes me for being impatient and impe-
rious. "Oh, these arrogant westerners!" he is probably thinking.
"They don't understand our culture." Startled and shamed by his
words, I heed his warning and lie low for the next few hours to
observe the proceedings.

Conference delegates include senior government bureaucrats
from different parts of Indonesia, community activists, leaders from
some of the largest non-government organizations (NGO's) in the
country, local and regional health representatives, and delegates
from international funders like the Ford Foundation and USAID. We

are at a location in the highlands of Central Java, and starting late is expected—*jam karet*, or elastic time as the Indonesians call it, gives everyone time to chat, renew old acquaintances and make new ones. Storytelling is in the air.

This scene took place over 20 years ago, but the details are still fresh for me: my embarrassment at being caught out in my ego-centricity, the colour and fragrance of sweet rice cakes wrapped in bright, green banana leaves, dark coffee so thick and sweet you could stand a spoon in it, and the babble in the conference hall. The participants have changed jobs in the intervening years, and I have changed personally as well, but the story remains vivid. This is my memory.

For the duration of the conference, delegates review the teaching case study I have prepared with colleague David Korten, then Asia Regional Advisor with the United States Agency for International Development (USAID).[52] The study examines the story of a primary health care project that has enjoyed success in this region. From modest beginnings 14 years ago, it has grown to become a model for delivering social services in a country strapped for funding. On the island of Java alone, there are more than 90 million people, and this presents the government with immense hurdles in terms of providing adequate health care for all. The attraction of the project under consideration is its grassroots and volunteer nature, making for cost-effective delivery and ensuring more accountability for providing health care within villages. As is often the case, after several years of rapid growth, the volunteers and the project seem to be losing steam. This conference gives us a chance to review the program and determine how it can be rejuvenated.

The formal proceedings finally get underway. Unmindful of clocks and schedules, these delegates will spend the rest of today and tomorrow narrating their respective experiences with primary health care provision, either as providers at the regional and local government levels, or as community development workers. The teaching case study will be a jumping off point for discussions about what needs to change.

To people familiar with Indonesian politics and culture, something profound is happening in the room. After 20 years of dictatorship under Soeharto, and ongoing distrust between the government and NGO community, people are finally talking. The NGO community has always represented a threat to the governing party under Soeharto. NGO's promote co-operative efforts and grassroots organizing. The government regards this as smacking of communism, which Soeharto brutally repressed in 1966, and it has been an uphill battle for the NGO community ever since.

There is a growing recognition in the capital that perhaps, after all, the government needs the NGO community to do things it can't. There will never be enough in government coffers to meet all the needs of a burgeoning population, and this conference is a step in building a rapport between the two sides.

Collaborating with David Korten as my mentor and co-author, I have developed a prototype for an organizational story that fits with the oral culture of Indonesian delegates. The country has a rich oral culture—stories abound on street corners, on buses, during meetings and celebrations. It seemed fitting that in performing a management consulting role, I too would use narrative techniques to write stories about organizations going through change.

A teaching case study resembles a wisdom story in its chronology. It sets out the story of how an organization came to be, the decisions and actions taken along the way, and where the organization is now. The various stakeholders review this story and debate what needs to happen next. In an ideal scenario, these parties include the organization under study, its peers, and government departments in whose jurisdictions it is active. The Ford Foundation in Indonesia has funded my research and facilitated bringing together conference representatives to discuss and debate the case study format. Our timing for introducing this prototype couldn't be better.

Indonesian NGO's have bitterly resented interventions in which international funding agencies parachute in western experts to find problems and make recommendations. The Ford Foundation office in Jakarta under the direction of Frances Korten (David's wife) has challenged this paradigm. Like their Asian counterparts in community development, David and Frances are convinced that grassroots participation is not just a passing fad; it is a necessary ingredient for the creation of sustainable communities, the kind that will outlast dictatorships and achieve more equitable development for people living at the margins in the developing world.

The actual case study format has evolved as a result of my meeting David Korten in Jakarta in the mid 1980's. David has been an advocate of people-centred development for some time and had just finished editing a book on the subject. He suggested we collaborate on the preparation of a teaching case study for use in the NGO sector. Early in his professional career, David taught at Harvard Business School using the case method of management instruction. His wife, Frances, wrote and taught management cases as part of their joint work on family planning program management. The format David and I have developed is an amalgam of the business and social science approaches, customized for the oral culture of Indonesia.

Our goal is to encourage participation from local and regional representatives, to make them part of the learning and decision-making. This perspective contrasts with the international funders' model, which favours western knowledge and expertise. We want to appreciate inherent strengths within local organizations in order to position them to achieve their goals.

The prototype for a teaching case study has married my three passions: a love of prototypical design, a conviction about participatory development and a delight in storytelling. Storytelling was definitely not on my original academic agenda. But as a student of architecture, I always preferred projects that engaged community participants in the design of their own spaces. Running through my studies was the theme of people-centred design.

This first conference has set the stage for more encounters between government and non-profit representatives in Indonesia. Future encounters will eventually lead to the creation of a ministry for cooperatives under the leadership of Adi Sasono, my boss at the Institute of Development Studies and a prime mover behind this conference. David Korten will go on to found the People-Centred Development Forum, and together with his wife Frances will serve with the Positive Futures Network, publishers of *YES! A Journal of Positive Futures*. I have the satisfaction of knowing that a story about a small NGO in the Javanese highlands has changed the world around it. Each time delegates meet, the story will be embellished and democracy advanced.

Storytelling can work in Javanese villages and it can work in multi-national workplaces. This is the power of story. ❧

Stand Up and Find Your Voice

If you don't tell the truth about yourself, you cannot tell it
about other people.

Virginia Woolf.

I MAGINE WORKING IN AN ORGANIZATION where your voice was
heard. Where it was safe to stand up for your values and speak
your mind. Not every suggestion or tip would be acted upon, but
you would feel your stories and ideas were taken seriously regardless of your rank at work.

In his participatory design workshops, Stan King asks participants to experience an environment with all of their senses. What
does it look? Smell like? How does it feel? You could ask the same
questions of a storytelling organization. Aside from the obvious
murmur of voices engaged in sharing narratives, what else would
you notice?

Storytelling organizations have cultures that value employee
participation. Examples are to be found in all sectors: non-profit,
institutional and corporate. A common characteristic is little or no
hierarchy. Training and development are high on the organizational
agenda, and employees are trusted with flex time arrangements.
Innovation is a by-product. Employee engagement scores are high.

The common element in coaching, mentoring, and sundry
participatory techniques is storytelling. It's a medium for strengthening community and communication, enhancing sustainability
and empowering employees to be accountable and find their voice

at work. Storytelling won't fix everything, but without it, all that can be heard is the organization's spin machine, or the click-clack of computer keyboards typing out the disenchantment of staff.

Belonging and accountability are twin results of the storytelling process described in *Find Your Voice at Work*. Individual employees need only be willing to share their stories and be open to the discoveries that come with exploring their personal narratives and listening to others. The organization's role is to accommodate employees' participation and facilitate learning and development. Bring these two groups together in an informal exchange for swapping stories and magic can, and does, happen. ❧

Summary VI

1. There are a variety of methods for introducing storytelling into an organization and making it relevant to current needs. Each method's success is predicated on the participation of employees in all phases of design and implementation.

2. Coaching provides an ideal entry point for storytelling and is most effective when coaches practice deep listening techniques that draw on the teller's experience rather than the coach's.

3. Peer mentoring is a self-directed learning process that enhances employees' retention of concepts. Each peer mentoring session includes opportunities for sharing stories about effective and ineffective workplace practices.

4. Storytelling is how people communicate in mentoring relationships. Encounters between mentor and mentee are fertile ground for the mentor to impart useful information about organizational life skills, such as dealing with tricky people dynamics.

5. Storytelling is traditionally an oral art, but the addition of visual imagery enriches dialogue between participants and is especially useful for envisioning a future state.

6. When it comes to leading with stories, a process of reflection, discussion and discovery enhances the development of solutions to the organization's challenges.

7. A teaching case study is the story of what an organization was like, what happened and what it's like now. It is most effective when wide representation from a variety of constituents—employees, managers, leadership, suppliers, peers, competitors and customers—is incorporated into the discussion and discovery process.

Afterword

"But *community* requires more than the sharing of stories—
true community requires the *discovery of a story that is
shared*. People 'sharing' their separate stories, no matter
how similar those stories may be, is not the same as *shared
story*. In this context, 'sharing' is not something that we
can create and control—it is something that *happens,* an
experience serendipitous and unbidden..."

Ernest Kurtz and Katherine Ketcham. [53]

The most memorable storytellers I have heard exhibited a peculiar
mixture of humility, courage, perseverance and gratitude.

- They have known enough adversity or made enough mistakes
  to be conscious of their own woundedness; this has made them
  humble.
- Living with difficult circumstances has made them courageous,
  even if they don't recognize it in themselves. If you were to quiz
  them about their bravery, they would probably refer you to someone else "who is really brave, not like me."
- They have a conviction about what matters in life and are determined to make a difference for those around them.
- Being able to see the light at the end of the tunnel has made
  them grateful. They often speak with gratitude of a supportive
  community.

Any one of these four factors is a good foundation for storytelling.
All four together make for powerful stories.

One of my projects in Indonesia took me into poor villages in
Central Java. There were numerous interviews to conduct in the short
space of a week, and I was impatient to complete the research so that

I could return to Jakarta and begin my report. The organizer for my field trip had suggested I attend a meeting late one afternoon between farmers in the area and the region's administrative authorities. The rationale for attending was not clear to me, so of course I resisted. My host prevailed and finally, to humour him, I agreed to go along. The encounter was held in a nondescript government office, with standing room only. It was hot and stuffy. The local bureaucrats were seated and looked comfortable in a middle class way. The farmers mostly stood, their faces weathered and their hands gnarled from heavy field work.

It was a long meeting in a predictably Javanese way but the storytelling was compelling. In this village the farmers were not voting for the dictatorship's political representatives, and as a result the environment had fallen into disrepair. Adjacent villages had money for upgrading roads and funding the construction of health posts and schools. Strangely there was no money to fund infrastructure needs in this village, not even provisions for primary health care.

When I attended this meeting more than 20 years ago, the average farmer in the Javanese Highlands lived in poverty, barely able to make ends meet. He had little or no formal education in the country's official language, Indonesian. Nonetheless, living in an oral culture had made this farmer articulate.

One by one, the farmers spoke to the village's impoverished status and the affect this was having on the farming community. Poor or impassable roads meant they could not get their produce to market on time. Failure to sell their produce spelled financial disaster. Their children were sick, the child mortality rate was high, and they needed better access to health care and clean water. If infrastructure improvements did not take place soon, they would be forced to migrate to Jakarta and abandon their farms.

The farmers openly acknowledged their political sympathies and their suspicion that failure to support the governing party's candidates in the last election had contributed to the administration's lack of support for basic infrastructure. To drive home their points, they narrated stories—stories about their homes, their village, and their way of life, all of which were threatened by the drought in services. Their manner was respectful but determined. Only a stone would have been unmoved by their plight.

These people lived with adversity on a daily basis. They did not sound sorry for themselves. Sustaining them and giving them hope were a combination of faith and the Indonesian practice of *gotong royong*, or mutual help in a community setting. The stories they told came from a deep place and resonated the more loudly for it.

I wish I could tell you that the heartfelt storytelling of these farmers was acted upon immediately. Change takes time, especially in a dictatorship. I imagine the farmers went home to anxious inquiries from their wives. "Empty promises", I can hear some of them saying. And their wives will have responded "Inshah Allah, God willing, something will be done to improve our situation." Every household in the village will have heard a version of the same story—*their* story of standing up for their principles and acting ethically in the face of government indifference and corruption.

In years to come, the farmers will narrate this story for their children, because children need to know their parents have done their best to care for them. Perhaps one day their children will tell similar stories of courage and perseverance. It remains to be seen whether they will share their parents' sense of gratitude and humility.

To embrace storytelling for the purposes explained in this book is to embark on a journey. Who knows where it will take you? The Mountain is a fearsome place but less so if you walk it with others. Find colleagues in your workplace or community who will join you on this storytelling adventure and together begin your ascent. I encourage you to dig deep along the way and to exercise a rigorous honesty in drawing on your personal experience for narrative content. Reflect on your mistakes just long enough to be humble and be grateful for what you have. And remember with each story to ask yourself: How can I make a difference today? ❧

Acknowledgements

The seeds for this book were planted in 2000 during exchanges I had with Vaughn McIntyre. Vaughn was launching Charity.ca and shared my enthusiasm for storytelling and the non-profit sector.

My passion for storytelling originally developed in Indonesia in the 1980's. Adi Sasono, then at the Institute of Development Studies in Jakarta, and Hasan Purbo at the Institute of Technology in Bandung, inspired me by their example as leaders and storytellers. David Korten at USAID and Frances Korten at the Ford Foundation in Indonesia encouraged my obsession by engaging me to develop a prototype for teaching case studies influenced by the Indonesian oral tradition.

Claude Lavoie, filmmaker and friend, urged me to devote my career to storytelling in the year before his death from AIDS. When he could not complete the project we had conceived, a video for social activist Dominique Machefert, two old hands in the business stepped in to help. Writer-producer Jude DeClercq and cinematographer René Collins guided me with patience and humour through the production of a story about the work of Servants Anonymous. That production experience in 2001 had a big impact on my storytelling skills, and convinced me that I needed to tell more stories about ordinary people making a difference in the world.

In 2002, Scott Knutson of Champion Technologies Ltd. hired me to collect stories from staff scattered at field locations in Western Canada. Corporate communications specialist Colleen Kozy accompanied me on my travels and modelled for me the kinds of qualities and competencies that everyone who tells stories ideally has: a willingness to listen, keep confidences, be integral, look for the best in others, challenge conventional thinking and never miss an opportunity to be entertaining.

My skill in storytelling owes much to support from colleagues at Toastmasters and the Canadian Association of Professional Speakers, Calgary Chapter. Natashia Halikowski, CoraMarie Clark, Garth Roberts, Mark Bernard, Betty Cooper, Kevin Clark, Mary-Ann Owens and others listened to my early efforts and helped me find opportunities for speaking. I am grateful for their coaching and confidence in my ideas.

Editor Fran Kimmel wholeheartedly endorsed the concept for this book and guided me in making it a reality. Several colleagues and clients contributed stories and ideas: Dennis Jensen, Patty Morris, Warren Redman, Cy Charney, Keith Seel, Jeff Nelson, Vaughan McIntyre, Kevin Clark, and Adam Battistessa.

Special thanks to all of the people whose stories lie within these pages and who are introduced to the reader only by their first names. I have appreciated their wonderful tales and support for this project.

The following colleagues either proofread parts of the text or challenged my ideas, to the betterment of the book: Ivan Zendel, Jacob Reichbart, Jocelyn Clayards, John Courtliff, Barbara Seedorf, Seva Terrell and Dr. Derrick Nolan.

At home, I have had daily inspiration from my son, James Allen, a born storyteller. My daughter Heather prefers hanging from ropes off cliffs, but is enjoying creating her own stories as a world traveller. Their faith and financial support for this project have been important to me.

Almost everything I have learned about telling wisdom tales in the last 16 years has happened in 12 step rooms. At last calculation, I have heard over 20,000 stories. A heartfelt thank you to members of the following groups for sharing their stories of experience, strength and hope: the Action Group, Getting There, Go For It and SMOG.

Andrée Iffrig, Calgary 2007

Reading List

Alexander, Christopher, Iskikawa, Sara, and Silverstein, Murray, *A Pattern Language*, Oxford University Press, 1977. Alexander's book is still the starting point for understanding the dimensions and qualities of people-centred communities. Each pattern is beautifully illustrated and explained.

Alternative Therapies, "Interview with Rachel Naomi Remen", May June 2006, Vol. 12, No. 3. Dr. Remen on the fear that keeps people from being "real".

Aristotle, *The Poetics*. Available in several translations and essential reading for anyone serious about the business of telling stories.

Atkins, Douglas G., "Review: (Inter)views: Cross-Disciplinary Perspectives on Rhetoric and Literacy, ed. Gary A. Olson and Irene Gale," *JAC* 12.2, 1992. Brief overview of Clifford Geertz' ethnographic writings on storytelling, seen from a rhetorical perspective.

Badaracco, Joseph L. Jr., "A lesson for the times: Learning from quiet leaders," *Ivey Business Journal*, Jan/Feb. 2003. Badaracco demonstrates that quiet leaders have much to teach us about the qualities of leadership.

Bridges, William, *Managing Transitions*, copyright Perseus Books Publishing, 1991. Bridges' insights into personal and organizational change are indispensable.

Cameron, Julia, *The Artist's Way*, Jeremy P. Tarcher/Putnam, 1992, 2002. Cameron has published several guides to self-development for creative people. *The Artist's Way* is a good starting point for anyone embarking on a journey of storytelling.

Carey, Benedict, "Have You Heard? Gossip Turns Out to Serve a Purpose," *The New York Times*, August 16, 2005. Carey's article makes the case for gossip at the office.

Chait, Richard P., Holland, Thomas P., and Taylor, Barbara E., *The Effective Board of Trustees*, Oryx Press, 1993. Chait, Holland and Taylor have established a framework for understanding the dimensions of leadership on boards in the non-profit sector, a framework with applications to the corporate sector.

Chait, Richard P., Holland, Thomas P., and Taylor, Barbara E., *Improving the Performance of Governing Boards*, Oryx Press, 1996. Follow up publication to *The Effective Board of Trustees*.

Chatwin, Bruce, *The Songlines*, Penguin Books, 1987. An evocative and spellbinding look at storytelling in nomadic cultures, written as a novel.

Cloke, Kenneth and Goldsmith, Joan, *Resolving Personal and Organizational Conflict*, Jossey-Bass, 2000. Cloke and Goldsmith bring insight and compassion to understanding victim narratives.

Denning, Stephen, *The Leader's Guide to Storytelling: Mastering the Art and Discipline of Business Narrative*, Jossey-Bass, 2005. This guide by Denning is aimed at senior leadership interested in using business narrative approaches in the organization.

Dryden, Ken, "Quebec and Canada: Our Common Story," *Maclean's Magazine*, Sept. 25, 2006. Dryden is a politician and former Hockey great who spins a tale to demonstrate that when we share our stories, we often discover we aren't so dissimilar after all.

Fulford, Robert, *The Triumph of Narrative: Storytelling in an Age of Mass Culture,* House of Anansi Press, 1999. Fulford originally prepared the content for the Massey Lecture Series. No collection on storytelling would be complete without this book.

Fulghum, Robert, *All I Really Need to Know I Learned in Kindergarten: Uncommon Thoughts on Common Things,* Villard Books, 1986, 1988. Classic collection of quirky tales from an accomplished storyteller. Fulghum demonstrates that you can be sincere and funny with your stories.

Geertz, Clifford, *Local Knowledge: Further Essays in Interpretive Anthropology*, Basic Books, 2000 and 1983. An erudite and entertaining study of the place of the observer/listener in hearing and transmitting stories, written by a pre-eminent anthropologist.

Ghandi, Unnati, "AIDS pandemic puts grandparents on the front line", *The Globe and Mail*, posted online August 12, 2006. Part of a series published by *The Globe and Mail* in 2006 for the International AIDS Conference held in Toronto, Canada. Wonderful examples of storytelling and how it can change the world.

Gladwell, Malcolm, *Blink: The Power of Thinking Without Thinking*, Little, Brown and Company, 2005. Master storyteller Gladwell muses about how we make decisions in this follow up to his bestseller, *The Tipping Point*.

Gladwell, Malcolm, *The Tipping Point: How Little Things Can Make a Big Difference*, Little, Brown and Company, 2000, 2002. Wannabe and established storytellers can glean much from Gladwell's approach to the writing of engaging narrative.

Goldberg, Natalie, *Writing Down the Bones: Freeing the Writer Within*, Shambhala Publications Inc., 1986. If you're serious about storytelling, buy this book. Goldberg's vignettes illustrate the "how-to" of writing and storytelling with a light touch, in no way detracting from the significance of the material.

Greengard, Samuel, "Stop Harmful Gossip Before It Affects Job Performance," *May Trends*, Vol. 26, No. 2. Greengard on how gossip undermines morale and productivity in the workplace.

Hamel, Gary, "Innovation as a Deep Capability," *Leader to Leader*, No. 27, Winter 2003. Hamel's ideas are explained in greater detail in the companion book, *Leading the Revolution*, Plume, 2000, 2002.

Honoré, Carl, "An Interview with Charles Handy, (Part One)," *Ivey Business Journal*, May/June 2000. Honoré conducted two interviews with British management consultant and iconoclast Charles Handy for the IBJ. Handy's quotes are irresistible.

Kenyon, Gary M., and Randall, William L., *Restorying Our Lives: Personal Growth Through Autobiographical Reflection*, Praeger Publishers, 1997. The authors show how to use storytelling to find meaning and be true to yourself.

Kimmel, Fran, "Office Gossip: How to Put a Lid on It," SAIT *Training Matters*, January 2005. Good overview of how to handle gossip in the office.

King, Stanley, Conley, Merinda, Latimer, Bill and Ferrari, Drew, *Co-Design— A Process of Design Participation*, VNR, N.Y., 1989. The work of Co-Design in promoting people's participation in development reminds that we have five senses, and visual expression is an important adjunct to the more cerebral exercises of talking and writing.

Korten, David C. and Klauss, Rudi, editors, *People-Centered Development: Contributions toward Theory and Planning Frameworks*, Kumarian Press, 1984. An early work by Korten and Klauss written for an audience in the field of international development.

Kotter, John P. and Cohen, Dan S., *The Heart of Change: Real-Life Stories of How People Change Their Organizations*, Harvard Business School Press, 2002. Kotter and Cohen provide a sound framework for understanding and planning change, with engaging stories throughout.

Kurtz, Ernest and Ketcham, Katherine, *The Spirituality of Imperfection: Storytelling and the Search for Meaning*, Bantam Books, 1992. Replete with dozens of wisdom stories, culled from Sufi, Hasidic and mystical Christian sources, as well as examples from Alcoholics Anonymous.

Locke, Christopher, Levine, Rick, Searls, Doc and Weinberger, David, *The Cluetrain Manifesto: The End of Business as Usual*, Perseus Publishing, 1999. Visit the website at *www.cluetrain.com* to learn more about the manifesto and its challenge to business as usual.

MacDonald, Margaret Mead, *Peace Tales: World Folk Tales to Talk About*, Linnet Books, 1992. Mead has put together a delightful collection of proverbs and tales that any workplace storyteller could use.

Olson, Gary A.,"Clifford Geertz on Ethnography and Social Construction," *JAC 11.2*, 1991. Another look at the writing of Clifford Geertz and the ways anthropologists approach the study and description of other cultures' customs.

Redman, Warren, *The 9 Steps to Emotional Fitness: A Tool-kit for Life in the 21st Century*, Merlin Star Press, 2003. Redman's book won the Award for Canadian Counselling Book of the Year in 2004; describes in detail how to apply his 9-step process for self-discovery.

Redman, Warren, *Recipes for Inner Peace*, Merlin Star Press, 2005. Redman takes *The 9 Steps to Emotional Fitness* and renders it as a series of short stories, with a little romance, food and hope thrown in for good measure. Both books explain his 5 step narrative cycle.

Remen, Rachel Naomi, M.D., *Kitchen Table Wisdom*, Riverhead Books, 1996. Physician and therapist, Remen has written a sublime collection of stories.

Remen, Rachel Naomi, M.D., *My Grandfather's Blessings*, Riverhead Books, 2000. Remen relates more stories in a moving appeal to encourage more authenticity and compassion in the medical profession. Her concerns apply equally well in the workplace.

Seel, Keith, and Angelini, Anita, *Strengthening the Capacity of Executive Directors*, Institute for Nonprofit Studies, Mount Royal College and Community Foundations of Canada, 2004. Seel demonstrates the use of a peer learning circle process.

Seel, Keith and Iffrig, Andree, *BEING A Governor: A Process for Board Development*, Institute for Nonprofit Studies, Mount Royal College and Volunteer Canada, 2006. The detailed templates in this publication would be useful for anyone embarking on peer learning. Download the booklet at *www.mtroyal.ca/nonprofit/governanceguide.pdf.*

Talbot, Michael, "Does Objective Reality Exist, or is the Universe a Phantasm?" *www.homepages.ihug.co.nz/~sa/hologram.html.* Talbot's life ended early, but this article together with his book on a holographic view of the universe are proof positive we continue to learn from him.

Terry, Robert W., *Authentic Leadership: Courage in Action,* Jossey-Bass, 1993. Terry's introductory chapters provide an instructive overview of an evolving understanding of leadership. His writing, research and community activism remain a source of inspiration for many.

Tufte, Edward R., *Envisioning Information,* Graphics Press, 1990. Information comes in many forms, of which stories are only one. Tufte's books and seminars illustrate how to take the dissemination and display of complex bits of information to new levels.

Welsh, Shona, *Mentoring the Future,* 2004. Welsh is passionate about her subject in this succinct book.

Yolen, Jane, *Dream Weaver,* Philomel Books, 1979, 89. *Dream Weaver* is one of more than 125 books written and/or edited by Jane Yolen. This collection contains several stories that lend themselves to short recitals.

www.torah.org/learning/halashon/intrtrue.html—a good introduction to Lashon Hara, or the subject of gossip.

Permissions

The following people graciously reviewed and allowed me to use their stories: Adam B., Arne J., "Barbara", Cathi D., Chris M., Colleen K., "Frank", Gary M., Jeff N., Rita E., Susan C.

Thanks also to Cy Charney, Kevin Clark, David Korten, Vaughn McIntyre, Patty Morris, Stan King, Warren Redman, Keith Seel and Harry Ulmer, who reviewed their stories to ensure accuracy.

Permission to quote is gratefully acknowledged from the following sources:

Louisiana State University Press, for the selection from *The Need to Hold Still: Poems by Lisel Mueller,* copyright © 1981 by Lisel Mueller.

HarperCollins Publishers, for the quote from *Gung Ho!,* by Kenneth Blanchard and Sheldon Bowles, copyright © 1998 by Blanchard Family Partnership and Ode to Joy Limited.

Graphics Press for the quote from *Envisioning Information,* copyright © 1990 Edward R. Tufte.

David Weinberger for permission to quote from *www.cluetrain.com,* website for *The Cluetrain Manifesto: The End of Business as Usual,* copyright 1999, Christopher Locke, Rick Levine, Doc Searls, and David Weinberger, Perseus Publishing.

Margaret Read MacDonald for permission to quote from *Peace Tales: World Folktales to Talk About,* copyright 1992 Margaret Read MacDonald, Linnet Books.

Alternative Therapies magazine, for permission to quote from "Interview with Rachel Naomi Remen," May June 2006, Vol. 12, No. 3, p. 93.

House of Anansi Press Limited for permission to quote from *The Triumph of Narrative: Storytelling in the Age of Mass Culture,* copyright 1999 Robert Fulford and the Canadian Broadcasting Corporation.

Gary Kenyon for permission to quote from *Restorying Our Lives: Personal Growth Through Autobiographical Reflection,* by Gary M. Kenyon and William L. Randall, Praeger Publishers, 1997.

Notes

INTRODUCTION

1. Floating Eagle Feather quotation from dedication page, *Peace Tales: World Folk Tales to Talk About* by Margaret Mead MacDonald, Linnet Books, 1992.

SECTION I

2. Robert Fulford, *The Triumph of Narrative: Storytelling in the Age of Mass Culture*, House of Anansi Press Limited, 1999, p. 9.
3. "An Interview with Rachel Naomi Remen," *Alternative Therapies*, May June 2006, Vol. 12, No. 3, p. 93.
4. Anthony J. D'Angelo. Founder of The Collegiate EmPowerment Company and creator of The Inspiration Book Series.
5. Gary M. Kenyon and William L. Randall, *Restorying Our Lives: Personal Growth Through Autobiographical Reflection*, Praeger Publishers, 1997, p. 33.
6. The material at *www.cluetrain.com* is also found in the book *The Cluetrain Manifesto: The End of Business as Usual*, by Christopher Locke, Rick Levine, Doc Searls, and David Weinberger, Perseus Publishing, 1999.
7. Found in *Peace Tales: World Folktales To Talk About*, by Margaret Read MacDonald, Linnet Books, 1992, p. 54.
8. John P. Kotter, Daniel S. Cohen, *The Heart of Change: Real-Life Stories of How People Change Their Organizations*, Harvard Business School Press, 2002.
9. Rachel Naomi Remen explores dealing with fear in *Alternative Therapies*, May June 2006, Vol. 12, No. 3.
10. Jane Yolen, *Dream Weaver*, Philomel Books, 1979, 1989, introduction.
11. Warren Redman, *Recipes for Inner Peace*, Merlin Star Press, 2005, p. 10.

SECTION II

12. Christopher Alexander, Sara Ishikawa, Murray Silverstein, *A Pattern Language*, Oxford University Press, 1977, pattern 129, p. 618.
13. I interviewed Larry Kwong for Asian Heritage Month celebrations in Calgary, Alberta in 2002. Kwong has also been the subject of newspaper articles and a video.
14. Warren Redman, *The 9 Steps to Emotional Fitness: A Tool-Kit for Life in the 21st Century*, Merlin Star Press, 2003, p. 10.

15. A former Executive Director of the DDRC, Patty Morris, shared these stories with me.
16. For an insightful look at the issue of gossip, c.f. commentaries on the Hebrew text, *Chafetz Chaim* by Rabbi Yisrael Meir Kagan of Radin, also known as the Chafetz Chaim.
17. Lisel Mueller, from the poem "Why We Tell Stories", *The Need to Hold Still*, Louisiana State University Press, 1981, p. 63.

SECTION III
18. Benjamin Mandelstamm, 19th century Russian Hebraist and author.
19. The doctor interviewed for the case study was Dr. Arif Haliman, then Executive Director of a social organization in Banjarnegara district in Central Java. Some of these vignettes are found in the *Final Report for the Workshop on Encouraging People's Participation in Regional Development (PPMP)*, prepared by the Secretariat for the Working Group on PPMP, Jakarta, 1987.
20. Hamel, Gary, "Innovation as a Deep Capability," *Leader to Leader*, No. 27, Winter 2003.
21. William Blake, *Auguries of Innocence*, 1803.
22. Talbot, Michael, "Does Objective Reality Exist, or is the Universe a Phantasm?" found at several locations on the web including *www.homepages.ihug.co.nz/~sa/hologram.html*. Here is the rose reference in its entirety: "If a hologram of a rose is cut in half and then illuminated by a laser, each half will still be found to contain the entire image of the rose. Indeed, even if the halves are divided again, each snippet of film will always be found to contain a smaller but intact version of the original image. Unlike normal photographs, every part of a hologram contains all the information possessed by the whole."
23. Dr. Derrick Nolan, Ivan Zendel, Ph.D., and Jacob Reichbart contributed to my understanding of the hologram and a holographic view of the universe.
24. Hillel, 1st century CE Rabbi, in *Pirke Avot*.
25. Found also in Anthony de Mello, *The Song of the Bird*.

SECTION IV
26. Robert W. Terry, *Authentic Leadership: Courage in Action*, Jossey-Bass, 1993.
27. Carl Honoré, quoting Charles Handy in "An Interview with Charles Handy (Part One)," *Ivey Business Journal*, May/June 2000, p. 55.
28. Joseph L. Badaracco, Jr., "A lesson for the times: Learning from quiet leaders," *Ivey Business Journal*, Jan./Feb. 2003, p. 5-6.
29. Carl Honoré, *Ivey Business Journal*, May/June 2005, p. 54.

30. "AIDS pandemic puts grandparents on the front line", article by Unnati Gandhi for *The Globe and Mail*, posted on August 12, 2006.
31. Shona Welsh, management consultant and author of *Mentoring the Future*.
32. Kenneth Blanchard and Stanley Knowles, *Gung Ho!*, HarperCollins Publishers, 1998, p. 2.
33. Ernest Kurtz and Katherine Ketcham, *The Spirituality of Imperfection: Storytelling and the Search for Meaning*, Bantam Books, 1993, p. 144-45.

SECTION V
34. Ernest Kurtz and Katherine Ketcham, *The Spirituality of Imperfection*, p.64.
35. William Bridges—American speaker, author and consultant on transitions. Author of several books, including *Managing Transitions*, copyright Perseus Books Publishing, 1980.
36. Robert Fulghum, *All I Really Need to Know I Learned in Kindergarten*, Villard Books, 1989, p. viii.
37. Rachel Naomi Remen, M.D., *Kitchen Table Wisdom*, 1996, p. xxix.
38. Clifford Geertz, *Local Knowledge*, 1983, 2000, p. 43. For other perspectives on Geertz' contributions to storytelling and rhetoric, c.f. Gary A. Olson's article in *JAC* 11.2 (1991) and Douglas G. Atkins' review of Olson's work in *JAC* 12.2 (1992), available online.
39. Joe Calloway, author and speaker, quoting Peggy Noonan, at a presentation for the Calgary Chapter of the Canadian Association of Professional Speakers, March 2003.
40. Harry Beckwith warns against the perils of criticizing the competition and overstatement in his Field Guide series: *What Clients Love, The Invisible Touch* and *Selling the Invisible*.
41. Mies van der Rohe, a revered 20th century German architect, and a founder of the Institute of Design, Chicago; in response to a question about why his buildings were so 'simple'.
42. From *Writing Down the Bones* by Natalie Goldberg (c) 1986, p. 100. Reprinted by arrangement with Shambhala Publications Inc. Boston, MA. *www.shambhala.com*.
43. Margaret Read MacDonald, *Peace Tales: World Folktales to Talk About*, 1992, p. 93

SECTION VI
44. Warren Redman, *The 9 Steps to Emotional Fitness*, Merlin Star Press, 2003, p. 32.
45. Shona Welsh, *Mentoring the Future*, 2004, p. 9.

46. Edward R. Tufte, *Envisioning Information*, Graphics Press, 1990, p. 9.
47. For readers interested in this topic, c.f. Christopher Alexander's seminal work, *A Pattern Language*, Oxford University Press, 1977, and Co-Design's guide to participatory processes, *Co-Design: A Process of Design Participation* (Stanley King with Merinda Conley, Bill Latimer and Drew Ferrari), 1989, VNY NY. David Korten has written extensively about voluntary participation. *Getting to the 21ˢᵗ Century, When Corporations Ruled the World*, and *The Great Turning* are some of his titles. He is the founder and president of the People-Centered Development Forum.
48. Keith Seel and Andrée Iffrig, *BEING a Governor: A Process for Board Development*, Mount Royal College, Institute for Nonprofit Studies and Volunteer Canada, 2006, p. 16.
49. Keith Seel's publications include *BEING A Governor: A Process for Board Development*, (with Andrée Iffrig); and *Strengthening the Capacity of Executive Directors* (with Anita Angelini), The Institute for Nonprofit Studies, Mount Royal College and Community Foundations of Canada, 2004.
50. For more information on the different dimensions of governance and leadership, c.f. Richard P. Chait, Thomas P. Holland, and Barbara E. Taylor, *The Effective Board of Trustees* and *Improving the Performance of Governing Boards*, Oryx Press.
51. David C. Korten and George Carner, "Planning Frameworks for People-Centered Development," in *People Centered Development*, edited by David C. Korten and Rudi Klauss, Kumarian Press, 1984, p. 201.
52. Andrée E. Iffrig and David C. Korten, *Banjarnegara and the YPPSE, Local Government-NGO Collaboration*. March 1987, part of a series, *Teaching Case Studies on the Strategic Management of Private Voluntary Development Agencies*: Published by The Institute for Development Research (IDR), Boston, Mass. and available through the National Association of Schools of Public Affairs and Administration (NASPAA), Washington, D.C., or through IDR.

AFTERWORD:
53. Ernest Kurtz and Katherine Ketcham, *The Spirituality of Imperfection*, p. 240.

About this book

Every book has a story, and *Find Your Voice at Work* is no exception. Meet the creative team who transformed the author's words into a book that reflects the generosity of spirit found in its stories.

Jacob Reichbart has many years experience in the print industry and book arts. He developed the online marketing strategy for *createbooks.com*, a web site for independent authors. He shares the author's vision of creating hospitable, harmonious workplaces. In creating the visual concept for this book, Jacob drew on typographic tradition, reflecting the enduring legacy of storytelling. He worked from concept through to production, ensuring that nothing was lost. Jacob has a background in architecture and product design. Learn more about his practice at *www.marketing-calgary.com/aboutus.html*.

Nieves Carrasco contributed the cover art. She is a fibre artist and graduate architect living in Toronto. Nieves and the author have known one other for more than 30 years, and share a love of textile art and great design. Nieves weaves stories with fibre, whereas Andrée uses words. Andrée owns some of Nieves' artwork, and when planning the book's cover, Nieves' images came to mind. Weaving and storytelling have much in common. To view more of Nieves artwork, visit *www.nieves.carrasco.com*.

Illustrator Merinda Conley is an artist and architect in Calgary. The author and she met as volunteer artists at Co-Design workshops in the early 1980's. For several years, Merinda headed the Alberta Main Street Program, and was responsible for supervising the renewal of 23 towns and city neighbourhoods. She has organized and participated in more than 200 public design workshops. When Andrée needed drawings of people interacting in the workplace, she approached Merinda to produce these. The result is a portfolio of illustrations with a folksy, story-like quality. Merinda is a consultant with her firm, Community Design Strategies Inc., email: *cds.inc@telus.net*.

Brian Smith and Mike McCoy of Articulate Eye Design were responsible for crafting Andrée's manuscript into a handsome-looking book. They listened to Andrée's expectations and Jacob's ideas and advanced some of their own, proving patient with a first-time author's anxieties. The result of their labours is a design and layout that owes much to traditional book design, harkening back to a time when people lingered over books and the stories in them. You can reach Brian and Mike at *design@articulateeye.com*.

Stories can be life changing

Use stories to:
- Solve problems in your organization
- Improve productivity and personal performance
- Communicate more effectively on projects
- Strengthen your organization's sense of community

Find Your Voice at Work is an integrated, 3-step approach to leadership and self-development for today's internet-savvy learner.

1. Read the book to be inspired by the power of storytelling. There are dozens of real stories from people who found their voices.
2. Subscribe to our online courses, learn more about yourself and begin a discussion about stories that matter.
3. Attend a discovery workshop to further develop your storytelling and communication skills.

Find Your Voice at Work is more than a book. It's the entry point for a series of books, online seminars and workshops designed to empower and engage employees. Swap stories with like-minded peers. Learn to use storytelling to build stronger workplace communities and stand up for what you believe in.

To learn more about finding your voice at work, visit *www.find-your-voice.ca*, or email *info@find-your-voice.ca*.

Limegrass Productions Ltd. designs and delivers training programs in leadership development.